D1523952

OTHER BOOKS BY MERRILL GILFILLAN:

Truck. Poems. Angel Hair Books, New York, 1970.

9:15. Poems. Doones Press, Bowling Green, Ohio, 1970.

To Creature. Poems. Blue Wind Press, Berkeley, 1975.

Light Years: Selected Early Work. Poems. Blue Wind
        Press, 1977.

River Through Rivertown. Poems. The Figures, Great
        Barrington, Mass., 1982.

Magpie Rising: Sketches from the Great Plains. Pruett
        Publishing/Vintage Books, 1988, 1991.

Sworn Before Cranes. Stories. Clark City Press, Livingston,
        Mont./Orion Books, New York, 1993, 1994.

On Heart River. Poems. Dayo Books, Denver, 1995.

Satin Street. Poems. Moyer Bell, Wakefield, R.I., 1997.

BURNT HOUSE
TO
PAW PAW

BURNT HOUSE
TO
PAW PAW

Appalachian Notes

Merrill Gilfillan

HARD PRESS, INC. 1997

A brief section of this book was published
in *To: A Magazine of the Graphic and Language Arts.*
Copyright © 1997 Merrill Gilfillan
Published in the United States by
Hard Press, Inc.,
a non-profit Organization:
P.O. Box 184
West Stockbridge, MA 01266

Gilfillan, Merrill, 1945-
  Burnt House to Paw Paw : Appalachian notes / Merrill Gilfillan.
    p.   cm. − (Profile Series ; 3)
  ISBN 1-889097-05-5 (alk. paper)
        Profile Series (Hard Press, Inc.) ; 3
F106 .G46 1997
917.404/43 21

ONE

I was reared in an Ohio town precisely on the edge of the Appalachian mountain system, a village located such that a drive to the west opens immediately onto the level land of glaciated prairie with bluestem waving here and there along the highway, while within a mile of the town limits to the east you are into something entirely different—the first roll and rise of the *hills*, and, eventually, a couple of hours to the southeast, the fold of the full Appalachians.

I marvel at the revelatory precision of that place-ment now more than I did back then, I am sure. But there was always a sense of that geographical inception that made the very word *Appalachian* hang brighter than it might have otherwise. It was a daily connection of sorts, with the sensation of standing at the foot of something, of standing on a conceptual beach just at breakers' edge.

And even now that is how I often get to the Appalachians: from my parents' home I leave town to the east with the unspoken but satisfying feeling that I am witnessing the whole thing. Within five minutes I am underway, climbing the range, from the first gully and buckle on up. Down the Licking River, through the plush, loamy moundbuilder country, curling up over Flint Ridge. . .

But it takes an hour or two to sense that one is into the *hills* proper. Nearing the Ohio River I watch for signals of the transition from outwash to foothill to mountain. The hills themselves grow larger and denser, but there is more subtle sign as well that announces the entry. A plowed field of a certain worn vermilion hue and the first stand of redbud trees blossoming in a low open hollow give trustworthy notice, along with the first handmade "Coondogs for Sale" sign on a telephone pole and the first coven of vultures dismantling a possum carcass beside the curving road berm. A man walking down the highway shows a certain ambling inward shyness in his gait, averts the bill of his cap to hide his face. There is an increase in abandoned pastures gone to brush and bramble, and people sitting on their springtime porches do so in a slightly unique way, an accomplished, familiar way that is perfectly private and yet social at the same time. Farther on, probably after crossing the Ohio River (a sensible but almost too easy boundary for the thing), there will be the first runaway truck ramp hacked out from the heavy woods, and, finally, the first footbridge, one of the surer indicators: a narrow plank bridge with cable handlines reaching 30 or 40 yards across a creek to connect an Appalachian home with an Appalachian road.

There is a heightening of the West Virginia accent on the ear and, more abstractly, there is a shift in mood and human context the farther one gets into the mountains. It is a rising of the nonhuman, of the silence and depth and sheer extent of the unoccupied Appalachians around and within all human activity, attitude, and intercourse.

But let's say, for this trip through, that our signal and emblem of Appalachian immersion is that distinguished old cast-off easy chair sitting at a gimpy tilt a few feet off the road in the very middle of a sunny blackberry tangle with the bushes in full ivory flower. That will do just fine. And now, with the sun straight up and the redbirds singing, we have officially entered what geologists call "the most elegant mountain chain on earth."

Two

The Ohio valley is astir with May. Farmers curry the wide, level melon fields and Carolina wrens exhort from roadside shrubbery. I hit the river at the hamlet of Fly and follow her downstream fifteen miles on the Ohio side. She is a formidable river from first glance, as always, low-slung and moody with a resentful, beast-of-burden cast to her even on fine days. I smell her heavy scent of muck and catfish water as soon as I edge her. On the far side the knobby green-up hills of West Virginia and a string of fluttery mirage habitations, glimpses of coiled cable and the gritty raw ends of riverbank commerce. A northbound coal train chugs export/import across a narrow bridge.

I stop for gas near the foot of the big bridge spanning to St. Marys, West Virginia, and go in to fill my coffee cup. The proprietor of the station is shooting the vernal breeze with a pair of old cronies in tight porkpie hats. I soon realize, as I sugar my coffee, that they are discussing the disastrous collapse of the Point Pleasant-Gallipolis bridge wherein some 50 people perished into the midwinter Ohio. That took place more than twenty years ago and some 70 miles downstream, but they jab and tack about the intimate details as if it were this very morning's news.

One old chap smacks his lips and declares, "There is a handful of other bridges up and down this river that will be going pretty soon if they don't watch 'em." I pay up and climb in the car thinking—"But not today!"

I cross into West Virginia and pass through the village of St. Marys and up the long steep switchbacked hill behind her to the ridgetop, the first of many hundreds, and drive south on Highway 16. Five miles in, I pull over at a high spot to let pushy traffic pass and to look off to the east, off and over at the great secrecy and fertile closure of the mountains and their hollows and runs, the soft hill upon hill, ridge after ridge, all buffered and screened by the beneficent canopy of broadleafed deciduous forest. It is always a surprise and an uplift, the first intimation of the magnitude, of the vast continuity of the Appalachians, their thousand miles of unbroken treetops bound and unified this very moment by the end-to-end overlap of countless titmouse songs.

There is a trace of haze and a cool moist silence this morning that shifts and sways like something palpable, adjusts with a slight flinch when a woodpecker calls. The aspect is long and imposing, yet comfortable; there is the knowledge that in the end these are traversable, walkable mountains. Unlike the Rockies or the Sierras, these ranges are conceivably crossable at almost any point, given the right shoes, a slicker, and a good snake stick. . .

Already the driving rhythm is set, the swing of the plumb and the shift and lean of the body through the curves. And already we are among the beautiful Appalachian ruins, the old houses given up and left to moulder on the slopes above the road. Ruins by tradition seem more poignant south of the Mason Dixon; they seem "heroically abandoned" in a manner that makes the sag of their rooves more eloquent and their broad porches loaded with junk and raccoon jetsam more reflective. Among the square and thrifty frame homes with admirable two-story porches and spring houses off to one side, their old unpainted barns starting to brown and curl, their sheds and shanties full of briars, listing among sumac, there are the classic mountain bungalows: one and a half story dwellings with house-wide low-hung porches with white posts and a host of chairs and half a dozen flower pots hanging from the eave lip. They are either white frame or red/brown tarpaper "brick." Some stand on cement block stilts—one in a creek bottom was set eight feet off the ground. All are tough and thin and sometimes feeble to the eye, and yet—this is the Appalachian patina—always, unabashedly, *sufficient.* And the many creekside housetrailers, even they are set parallel to the road with the ubiquitous wide porch and roof rigged to them such that the entire structure closely resembles the bungalows of the preceding generation.

At the edge of Burnt House I stop for lunch, pulling up a sharp gravel drive to a churchyard. A Methodist church, it says above the door, built in 1889. It stands, painted neatly white, amid a grove of mature oaks and commands a short but handsome view: a brushy draw runs below, beyond Highway 47, and to the north a narrow dirt road disappears up the mountain side, just eking out a path of least resistance through the trees. A small graveyard lies on a terrace a few feet above the church parking lot, and then a spanking white outhouse, its two doors labeled "Adam" and "Eve."

I get out of the car to stretch and make a sandwich on the hood and quarter a big dill pickle lengthwise. There are crows yelling away up that enticing little dirt road and the bluejays in the church oaks cock an ear to listen. When I turn back toward the church I discover a man peeking at me around the corner of the building. A tall pale man of 60 in Oshkosh overalls, he bends timidly from the waist, out from behind the corner, his head under a navy blue ballcap waggling with a will of its own over his hesitant frame. He is possessed, it appears, by amentia; maybe a caretaker at the church: pew-polisher and fly swatter. I take a step in his direction, thinking to say hello, explain my presence, but my sandwich-in-hand does that, I guess, and the fellow shrinks, and the waggling intensifies, so I stop and turn back to my car and finish my lunch trying to make myself unobtrusive and harmonious, gazing off into the upper oaks.

* * *

I am taking this long misshapen ride through my own country for a rest and for a classic change of scenery. And for a certain healing, for refuge amid the chlorophyll after a brush or two with the dark side. I want to sit in the Smoky Mountains at warbler time.

Homeland travel is a different proposition in many complicated, less-than-obvious ways from international travel. In France or Mexico, or Canada for that matter, the situation is clear-cut to all involved: a person from elsewhere is nosing around, and what he or she sees is bound to be foreign and stroboscopically highlighted, touristically framed. But in West Virginia or outer Texas the relations are less simple. The equation can sometimes curdle. An obviously native traveler—one who loiters and looks twice and even thinks about what he sees—can arouse suspicion in local inhabitants, as if an appraising eye cast on one's own country is somehow presumptuous or ungrateful or subversive. On the other hand, the carpetbaggery and easy transient thievery latent in a complaisant domestic glimpse can be legitimately irritating to people who know a place in

17

depth. Thus in the end it can be awkward, even disagreeable, the moment when one is discovered lingering on someone else's bridge extracting the poetic juices from someone else's river, raiding their hometown honeycomb.

So at Burnt House I try to gather my wits and key my eye to make this Appalachian swing an honest passing through; more than simple, glancing motion. I seek the company of vast green reaches and constant bird song, and a certain mending of the *what-gives*. Let me shake all inordinate carpetbaggery and tune to the given lapidary of elemental days-in-place; let the looksee be clear and mutual and light.

Laurence Sterne, odd landscapeless traveler, catalogued his fellows in classes such as the Inquisitive traveler, the Proud traveler, the Lying, the Vain, the Splenetic traveler, as well as the common Simple (or Commercial) traveler. There are, since Einstein, scores of candy-store variants and mutations. The gill-breathing, the persiflage, the deconstructivist, the local coloratura traveler.

Basho, the Poetic traveler, wandered about bejewelling the passage of time and the fragility of the human edifice. Nowadays the shrill push of the species and its fin-de-siècle muddle, its edifice ranging from rank to rampant, sometimes threatens even that wistful cello accompaniment to the looking. But not to give in to the Splenetic traveler: This time through the

Appalachians it will be the old standby Lonesome traveler, with capacity and rights reserved to accelerate into the Ghostly traveler, or decelerate into the Stray-dog traveler, lolling in the sun when the time is right.

There is each day in all directions up and down the road inextinguishable amazement at the virtuoso tenacity of botanical nature and the beauty of women along the way.

From Burnt House, now that I am well into the mountains, I drop south and then sharply southwest to commence my vaguely oriole-nest-shaped journey. I turn on the radio and jimmy in a weak area station and settle in for the afternoon. A man with an oily reverential voice is soliciting $18.00 a month from his true listeners to support orphans, or, if you prefer, lepers. But today a fresh matriarchal breeze is blowing and down below Tanner people are out enjoying the day, stand talking nice and easy near the road. Laundry flaps on clotheslines and the work goes on. An old woman bends in a cemetery, scrubbing a tombstone with water bucket and sponge; a woman and a young girl mysteriously drag a rocking horse along a rural forest edge.

Within an hour I am restless, I need to get out of the car, so I stop at Grantsville and drive around until I notice River Street, and turn down that rutty way skirting the edge of town where it fronts the Little Kanawha. I park in an unobtrusive place between rubbley store-backs and the drop of the river bank and open the door and lean back. I have a touch of a whiskey head from the bon voyage party and the warm lull of the alley is calming. The stream is muddy and high from recent rains. I hear her clatter and clip along. Beyond her a steep wooded ridge rises. The backside quiet of the town feels as good as the sun. A Kingfisher rattles down the river and from across the way a distant lapdog yaps from a hidden hollow; it echoes and bounces four-fold down the hill.

I remember the first real excursions I made into these mountains. 1964. I was 18 and came down with a friend from college in a black Volkswagen. We drove like crazy to the Rolling Stones and Supremes, slept on the ground anywhere we pleased or put up at fleabag tourist rooms through Kentucky and West Virginia and all the way to Asheville, North Carolina, everything washed with the creamy new-light of the first look. We loved the hawk-wild tangle of it, its mythic otherliness, and the headstrong maze of its twisting back roads. We stared in disbelief at our first red-eye gravy. We passed a pretty teenage girl somewhere in remote West Virginia—she was wearing a breezy old-fashioned plaid dress and walking downvalley along the railroad tracks with her head down in maddening self-containment. We talked about her for weeks, and knew full well that she was the Truth of the Matter. Recollected, the entire

20

trip has a custardy Thomas Hart Benton musculature.

But this afternoon in Grantsville it takes a few minutes of backalley sun to cut into that blossom and core,
to step out of the disposable hum and commercial
falsefront lining the highways and into the gist of it all;
but that will come when it is ready. I splash canteen
water on my face and walk around into the main street.
It is a compact business district with handsome stone
buildings around the pivotal courthouse square. The
downtown is bustling with shoppers; pickup trucks with
red mud splashed high on their flanks sit waiting along
the curbs with grannies lean as Ghandi in them.

I go into a busy cafe for carryout coffee. It is a
strange, out-of-kilter place with easter-egg purple walls
adorned with a tacky hodgepodge of ornaments and
tassled curtains where there are no windows that
reminds me instantly of an odd-ball sprang-up-
overnight "Indian" restaurant in New York City. Then
I roll on south and soon hit Route 33, a major east-west
artery, and follow its thin valley-trickle of human habi-
tation west. There are crisp white churches set on lovely knolls among the woods. Family groups in old cars
tear by, several generations within exuding a voracious
holiday-like wonder. Small roads digressing from the
highway into the hills smack of things like ham and
greens or biscuits with cocoa gravy. Huge rock ledges
hang at the lip of the valley; one large chunk has torn
off and fallen and landed directly on some sort of

home or roadside shack: a few splintered boards extend from under the edges, like feathers on a cat's jowls.

I cut south at Spencer. It is too much to try and hold the curving road, fend off local dervish drivers, and write at the same time, so I jump off at Gandeeville, picking a lesser road from the map, and bear up the long eight-mile hill toward Harmony, West Virginia, to dawdle at will.

The road is paved but very narrow and climbs steadily through patchy woods and wide pastureland. Two highschool girls are in their yard practicing a snappy marching band routine with large green flags; they freeze shy and giggling as I pass. Beyond the isolate Harmony post office the road forks, then dwindles; the countryside is higher and more still. The route is finally a one-lane track threading its way through woody curves and occasionally right through farmyards—chickens squawk and dash out of path in a Ma Kettle-style flurry.

And then for three miles at the bulging top of the mountain it is raw dirt, creeping along above steep drops and through bald peak pastures with long hazy vistas over Roane and Kanawha counties. Twice I stop to put the binoculars on irresistible specimens of hinter mountain houses, humble hundred-year-old white frame homes set in May-green glades just where the hollows narrow and the forest rises. And there, high above river level, admiring the cachet of these deep-rooted dwellings in the sun, I feel the kick-in and quick *frisson* of breakthrough (the body entered the Appalachians just north of the Ohio River, and now, somewhere between Harmony and Kentuck, West Virginia, the inner life has caught up): they are full of broad axes, zithers, and mayapple jelly.

THREE

I camped that night in a West Virginia state park whittled from a stream valley. For supper I heated up a quart Miracle Whip jar of homemade chicken and noodles I bought earlier at a church bake sale back in either Hamlin or West Hamlin. I ate them at a wooden table carved ridiculously deep with lovers' initials. I tried to calculate what stream I was sitting beside, but the maps of these mountains are so crowded with topo features and village names it is difficult to pin things down. I considered writing a line on the miraculous redbud trees—but the waterthrushes were singing close at hand. And I was content just to be there, inside the mountains, *within*.

* * *

Over the past century and a half the Appalachians have been many things in the non-Appalachian American mythos: an undisturbed romanticized pocket of essentially 18th Century speech and folkways; a nest of incest and moonshine whiskey; a benevolent playground for coastal planter families; a textbook study-ground for the case of "environmental determinism"; a hard-pressed setting for the post-World War Two psychoanalytic paradigm of dense Calvinist hot-poker convolutions of guilt and denial, wherein overworked dour women resent their domineering speechless men and stiff-necked men congregate to sing falsetto and sad—even womanly. In any event, it is sobering whimsey to consider eastern North America without the Appalachians; to imagine driving from Cincinnati to Richmond, Virginia, over one long straightaway past countless burgher-farmers and their well-groomed level lawns and cozy granary shadows. As these mountains were the first barrier to colonial surge and the westerly spread of commercial civilization, so they are now a relief from both homogeneous, manageable topography and the calcified docile mind.

I recall a moment on a New York City-bound Greyhound bus years ago that shed some light on the Appalachians, at least to a callow lad. It was just daybreak and we were rolling somewhere in central Pennsylvania, in the mountains, and a middle-aged man with considerable road dust on him scratched his head yawning and said as he gazed sleepily out the window: "If I didn't know better I'd think I was in southern Mexico."

And right he was; they have that very look to them, the wildness and texture and implication of the uplands of Guerrero. Once across the Ohio River they all become, I suppose, officially mountains, but they are usually *hills* to the people within them—*hills*, as in the Cheviot or the Wicklow hills in the old countries—

the affectionate diminutive full of an entire lifeway and world, a culture as intact and well-defined as any regional culture on the continent, complete with its own speech and music and deep sense of sanctuary that amounts to love and accounts for the fabulous homesickness of its emigrants, the hillward glances and fierce longing of its outlying pockets in Detroit or Cincinnati, and the intense nostalgia of its song. Grown men in bars on Columbus' Parsons Avenue stare deep into their beer and their jaw muscles clinch when someone on the juke croons for eastern Kentucky.

It must be the enwrapping privacy of the hills (there if you want it) that inspires such attachment, in combination with family of course and the beauty of the land. But these latter can fail with the turn of the seasons and the squawks of the heart; the sanctuary and cushioning of the hills will not—the sanctuary resonant with pre-social thought pools and spirit-spoor of how many centuries, pure and lost and glady enough to connect with Thracian satyrs or Dravidian woods dancers.

Cool, sweet, walkable hills where you might wander all day minding your own, or gobbling like a turkey if you want to. They come to be the touchstone of true, worthwhile life for hillpeople. Over the past hundred years migrants from the Appalachian core have wandered, when things got crowded or the itch took hold, but usually they moved with one thing in mind: sweeter, more private, hardwood hills. They eddied northwest as far as the hills went, into southern Indiana. Some stayed there, others moved southwest down the Ohio valley. A few, with a bad case of *the hills,* made the jump over to the Ozarks in mid-19th Century for a last bonanza in northern Arkansas; where they tuned their fiddles and sang of Tennessee.

* * *

Next day, I cross the Big Sandy River into Kentucky and go south, jumping off on little Route 9 ascending the Tug Fork. The morning is full-rigged and the road is scenic, winding its narrow way beside the river with low morning sunlight beaconing the forest, dazzling the eye with its many colored snakeskin-dapple and leaf-calico. The stream is lined with lovely sycamores, their bright pinto adding to the woodland shimmer. Of all the endemic beauties of the eastern continent the sycamores are paramount; it would be as hard to design a more striking tree as it would be to design a finer warbler than the Cape May. They evoke cool streambottoms across the middlewest, their pale, soft-palette reflections awrinkle in the deep smallmouth pools; in October their fallen leathery leaves shoal and drift on sleepy creeks and rivers.

I can picture the first sycamore I notice on drives east across the country, a welcome one just outside Junction City, Kansas. From there on they are regular, so handsome in their alabaster that farmers traditionally spare them in the bottomland fields from Missouri to Ohio—they stand, venerable lone survivors of the mass cuttings. Their white and olive bark hints of great esthetics far beyond the mandrill's arse; is cool to cheek and arm.

I park along the Tug Fork and walk over to see the stream. There, below the titmouse calls in the awakening woods, shine the three dominant whites of this May Kentucky left bank: the train of sycamores, the twinkling dance of the many dogwood blossoms, and the drifts and talus of decades of human trash—milk jugs, diapers, cans and mattresses, washers, dryers, frigidaires—dumped over the lip of the stream.

I creep through Beauty and Pilgrim and Lovely, Kentucky, just before the bridge takes me back into West Virginia at Kermit. Immediately south of that town the presence of coal begins to make itself known. There is black coal dust on the berms of the highway and scattered chunks of the stuff at pull-off areas. Coal trains sit loaded and waiting along the road and the big tough coal trucks roar by with increasing frequency; and, there, one overturned on its back in the ditch like a huge tortoise.

Somewhere below Nolan I stop at a rural road-house for a sixpack of beer and a cordial exchange about the weather. On the payphone just outside the front door an eighteen- or twenty-year-old coal boy is talking to his girl. He leans lank and shirtless against the wall, jeans low on hips, his slim upper body and curly dark hair—Mick Jaggerish in its morph and trim—streaked with coal dust, a faun for some would-be Appalachian pinup calendar.

Late afternoon I reach Williamson, West Virginia, still on the Tug Fork of the Big Sandy, and stop for the day. The town is jammed in along the river and among the hills and feels a bit pinched, hard to negotiate at first. I finally get directions to a motel from a friendly young man on the street who oddly manages to wrap up his information with a shuffling apology for being "just a taxi driver."

In the motel room, there is a long cigarette burn on the Gideon Bible. The proprietors send me down-town to King's Diner for supper, a plate of cornbread and beans. The waitress calls me "honey."

Then I take a stroll along the main street and hap-pen onto the "House of Coal," a small building now housing the Chamber of Commerce, I think it was, built of local coal blocks in 1933, glossy seam-coal, bright and varnished looking, corny as a butter castle or an ice capade. But this is the heart of the bitumi-nous country—Pike County, Kentucky, across the river,

30

has often been the number one coal producing county in the states—and back at the motel talk with the owner turns that way. He talks about the local violence during a major strike two years ago, the UMW versus A. T. Massey; the bad stuff up on Blackberry Mountain, when people got shot and there were sandbags in the streets of Williamson, they say; and bullet-hammered doors and prowling security forces and rumors of private armored vehicles growling through the pinching streets. The motel maids found pistols and Bowie knives under pillows. There were tense moments at a crosstown establishment when a major bureaucratic snafu bedded federal cops and UMW officials and hired mine-goons all under the same motel roof. The motel owner told me about the funeral procession of one truck driver who was killed—175 coal trucks out this very highway from Williamson; the victim's brother drove the shot-up truck behind the coalblack hearse.

Sour mountain music up along Turkey Foot and Blackberry creeks. . .

Back in my room I break the frequency and drink a beer while browsing in the local phonebook. These hills are full of rare, holdout Christian names. And this is homage, not carpetbaggery: Many of these names— old, quasi-biblical, and handmade custom jobs—might well be riding out their final incarnations, the last go-round for certain Anglo-syllable compounds. I have a similar list from my own native county in Ohio—first-names like Corlis, Doit, Lemoine, Nerol, Estile, Cunard, Galand, Goorley, Alon, and Fleet; Ova, Veldron, Nary. In the Williamson book I find the following (given names only): Vadis, Hassel, Conard, Oma, Athalean, Pricy, Ermel, Jenis, Daris, Vicy, Otha, McQuedis, Ganio, Pearlis, Lancle, Muncy, Lona, Persilla, and Salo.

They are, many of them, pleasantly Shakespearean on the ear, good to drop off to sleep by.

FOUR

I watch the ash trees through the year because Gerard Manley Hopkins watched them. I study and mark the tiny "whale-tongue" of the infant leaf-sheath, that type-pod with its Haidaesque "men-in-canoe" arch-density and formation; the thick-working-finger *spang* of the winter crown whorl; and the humble upreach and salmon-hued curve of the terminal twigs. I watch for the inscape so dear to Hopkins' heart.

Long after Negative Capability and Dialectical Materialism jelled and clarified and were filed away, inscape and its instress remain, elusive and beckoning. When I consider Buckminster Fuller's prophecy that "twenty-first century man will be preoccupied almost entirely with scientific and poetical research," I envision inscape studies high on the latter hill.

I read Hopkins' journals more than his poems, of late, for the simple sensory register, for the stamp of those English days. I see him paused along a path on a breezy afternoon, his rufous hair ruffling, looking, as always, looking long and steady with his mild centripetal gaze. Always and everywhere, the intense, devotional registry—up at the sky, across the meadow, down the valley. "I looked at the peacocks." "I was looking at high waves." "I looked at the pigeons in the kitchen yard."

What kept him so raptly looking was the endless possibility of discovering inscape. It is a concept best approachable through example. W.A.M. Peters defines it as "the outward reflection of the inner nature of a thing"—the principle giving any object its delicate uniqueness of form. The essential energy of being, by which all things are upheld in their particular inscapes, Hopkins called instress. Instress is the dynamic of inscape, and includes the process of perception and recognition in the observer. It is an illumination of pattern, of type-law, as carried by the individual object. And finally, to set it all back down on the maple table, "poetic creation occurs when the poet's own inscape is instressed by a complementary inscape in nature. The resultant poem is therefore a *new* inscape."

Inscaping is a process and crystallization of contemplative observation and visual mull. For Hopkins it was a critical weave in the Christ-world; but even without that programmatic leap it leads to an on-going, mandalic relation with the details of one's world, a patterned world as rich as (and perhaps more firmly based than), say, that of William Blake.

Hopkins found it almost everywhere—it has a pleasant latent pantheistic side. In animal and vegetable realms, and in the so-called inanimate realms of wind and saltwater. In a stand of Swiss trees; in an alluvial fan seen from afar; in "fine flue clouds inscaped in continuous eyebrow curves"; in snow on leafless elms

("It restored, to the eye, the inscape they had lost"); in bluebell droop and chestnut blossoms and a spray of ash; in sea surf (he tried to "unpack the huddling and gnarls of the water and law out the shapes and the sequence of the running"); in the slow growth of irises in 1868, in which the successive stages from bud to flower were noted as "sidings" of a single inscape. He found it in the human, as well. Castle ruins and certain strokes of architecture evoked the earthly, often inadvertent, *fit* of things, as did a distant footpath—its curious poignancy and inevitability verging on predestination—broken through new morning snow.

It is an alternative reading and decoding of the sensory world. It leads from *savoir* to *connaître*, from *écouter* to *entendre*. It slows the eye and heightens detail and is, accordingly, a radical, nonacquisitive contemplation, a dulling of the fang.

Since I was 20 the concept has teased me. For a quarter century I have watched for it, angled for it, gone running back to Hopkins on occasion for advice. There have been moments of wash-out and high moments with the sense of impending breakthrough. I watched stands of tall prairie sandreed rocking in the wind, the like curvature of the blond stems, "rocking in a *gestalt-scape;* waving in brilliant species circumscription, in unalterable sheer *occurrence.*"

I looked at a grove of perfectly symmetrical tulip trees in an Ohio woodland, each individual rising in two elegant mirror-image boles from a fork near the ground, and wrote, "Inscape as revelation of *form* within *vector,* of the One within the Many. Inscape as visible principle; a pre- and post-logical evidence of species-design." And, one January dawn, from a train in eastern Nebraska: "Awoke to sudden new inscape mass of bare large oaks: *seeing* it: the configuration of the biomass in such a stark, dumb, near-inevitable beauty and humbleness of intent and near-will that it is elative and unmistakable: creaturedom revealed at its raw root: the oak *signature,* gestalt-chord, primal image fundamental as Christ on the cross, an archetypal image of *Soit. . .*"

But I suspect that if a breakthrough comes it will come with the return of the warblers one May. These mountains are alive with warblers in a density that is almost giddying. I roll down the car window to hear them singing in the woods as I drive. This morning I found a Black-throated Blue dead on the Tug Fork road—they are that abundant—and went back for a once-in-the-lifetime look in hand. Lovely, just up from the Indies, tiny as a wet mouse.

Warblers on the retina work like honeysuckle on the nose. During migration, when the stream valleys are full of them, it is total immersion. To be under the right tree on the right morning of May is to partake of one of the great biomagnetic fields, a rush of such delicate beauty and intensity that it is best described as tidal, as a wave—a wave by Hokusai.

I had the good fortune to know them as a boy, thanks to family teachings, and the base-imprints for many of the fancy warblers are set there, in Ashtabula County, Ohio—Black-throated Greens dangling in the new-leaf treetops along the Grand River; Cape Mays browsing among apple blossoms in the Satin Street yard. After a ten-year hiatus I rediscovered them at age 30 in Riverside Park, New York, one spring day when I looked up to see an ornamental crabapple ajitter with a flock ascending the Hudson. That night they were in my dreams again.

Each winter, latter January or Candlemas, when the light has turned, and the owls, but not much else, I begin to think of them just stirring in the tropics, their colors brightening and the restlessness setting in. From that point on, I am waiting. I pull down the A. C. Bent *Life Histories of North American Wood Warblers* or Frank Chapman's *Warblers of America* and read a snatch now and then while the snow blows—a paragraph on the winter haunts of the Black-poll or migration routes of the Cerulean. Just a taste to rekindle the good, the planetary sumptuous.

Or, one cold clear February day I will walk out to a favorite warbler spot along Whetstone Creek and stand for half an hour in the empty woodlands. The stream is the color of cafe au lait and running high. I get in to

37

the lee of a big spruce and look up at the bare sycamores and the grapevine tangles that in three months will be busy with warblers and in the odd off-season stillness I think of them readying in Guatemala or Honduras and consider (for a brief moment) the notion of "calling them in" in the fashion of shamans of yore, specialists with the power to summon creatures from afar to ease the needs and hungers of their people.

By the second half of April I will be back, still waiting, standing quietly amid the young mayapples and wild ginger, watching the treetops just ahaze with tiny leaf-points, waiting for the first gnatcatcher whine that will signal the opening of the migratory gates.

And then one morning they are there in force, as they are here now in Appalachia. A Black-and-White in the elm, then a Canada, and higher up a flurry of Chestnut-sideds. Parula, Cerulean, Magnolia—a Blackburnian in the box elder. And for hours and days they will be there, flowing through, small things at large on a dangerous planet, birds of exquisite color and miraculous design, half a continent quick with them, brightened and gladdened before your very eyes.

To visualize the flock as perennial tumbling Möbian *front* is to catch the tidal inscape and all the watercycle beauty of its species-drive and myriad particulate summonings. It is bio-electric event on the scale of sunrise and whales breaching.

How long has the Chestnut-sided Warbler looked the way it does this mountain morning? Forever is a close enough guess. Inscape it on that buckeye blossom against eight- or nine-hundred dewy Mays. A formal, eye-of-the-beholder, urgent, sun-struck wave. A wave by Hokusai.

FIVE

I spent an hour in Pikeville, Kentucky, in the spring of 1983 and left town in a state of real wonder. The place struck us, then, as the epitome of the insular Appalachians. The concrete curbs along the narrow streets were three feet high, broken here and there with awkward steps to the sidewalks. The considerable traffic—largely pickup trucks and barnacled American gunboat-cars—crawled in a methodical bumper-to-bumper procession around and around the counter-clockwise one-way thoroughfare encircling the central downtown. People in the streets had the look of a populace apart, as if the rudimentary metropolitan light hurt their eyes; their speech was hard to follow. Slow; on the dusty side; around and around—undeniably an urban vortex for the area, there was still something so otherly, so floating third-world. . . *Like Mexico.*

This time through it is quite different. It looks almost urbane. Something has changed in the past decade. I stop to visit a root-and-herb buyer on a lesser road just outside town. "Botanicals Since 1900." The business is housed in a modern metal building with large bay doors for trucks to load. Bulging gunny sacks lean along one wall. The air holds a faintly acrid essence-of-sylvan aroma. On the counter in the office area specimens of dried herbs and roots are displayed.

The manager tells me his company—it has another branch office in the North Carolina mountains and one in the Ozarks—handles more than 2,000 different herbal products, from tiny pen-knife shavings of root bark and dried blossoms to hand-sized rhizomes and burlap bags of leaves. All plucked far up the hollow or on the isolate ridgetops by men and women in plaid flannel shirts with a pillowcase sack over one shoulder.

Most of the botanicals go to the major pharmaceutical companies like Upjohn and Lilly. Some are purchased by homeopathic doctors. Among the eighty-some items listed on the current price list, Balm of Gilead buds will bring $1.50 a pound, dried Bloodroot $2, Mayapple root 50 cents, and dried Witch Hazel leaves $1. Shonny haw bark brings 65 cents, walnut hulls a dime, Queen of the Meadow 80 cents. One of the highest (short of ginseng) is Black Culvers root, for which the company pays $8 per pound.

A quiet man in a briar-foxed hunting coat has just brought in 40 pounds of wild yam root he has gathered and dried over the winter and is paid $28 for it. Business is brisk, but before I leave the manager shows me a dried root cluster, light as cork, that greatly resembles a desiccated buffalo chip. It is Stone Root, he tells me, *collinsonia canadensis*—sent to California and "used in Preparation H."

This morning I drove over through Matewan, West Virginia, and Red Jacket, past Mary Taylor Mountain and into Taylorville. Skinny foxhounds trotted along the little road and in Taylorville there was a fine old relic of the "Delbarton Boxing Club," a storefront now a repair shop, with an old mural of a Dempsey-style boxer with his dukes up.

The little valley hamlets, like Hardy, extend along the highway for a mile or more, one-house deep on either side of the road, the porches of the homes just a yard from the curb—a simple social modality, like people waiting for a parade—then it is back into the forest and the twinkling dogwoods and the redstart songs and now and then the little churches in their glens. Coal trucks were constant on the winding roads, as were electioneering posters, many of which, I finally registered, touted Hatfields for sheriff and McCoys for constable, or the other way around. Then, in the village of Matewan, a historical marker told me that this was indeed the very turf of all that legendary fussing; the Tug Fork was the boundary between the two clans. Above the village, several tiers of train track were chiseled onto the steep hillside, stacked almost vertically, with coal trains in waiting.

* * *

43

Eastern Kentucky and southwestern West Virginia were the last regions in Appalachia to be settled. Up until the big bituminous boom of the 1870s, this was the wild place. Harry Caudill, in *Night Comes to the Cumberlands,* recounts the settling of the region with a starkness that is sometimes protested for its harsh summary vision: It was first populated (in Euro-terms) just after the Revolutionary War by shaggy people from the eastern Appalachians (the Blue Ridge area) who were feeling unwelcome population pressure as that territory filled up. It was a radical breakaway move for them into utterly uncharted country. Eastern Kentucky was thus settled, around 1790-1800, by this singular type of displaced, Appalachian-born generation from just over the mountains, a rankled people who strongly preferred the raw frontier state to any transition to comfort and good neighborliness. Caudill paints them as fierce outcasts and ex-felons, mean and wood-wise and proud of it, the products of half a century of complete isolation, a hellcat, unruly offspring of entirely illiterate lineage.

This, with all its sullen karma, is what the unfortunate native peoples of the inner Appalachians faced: white tribes remarkable not so much for their historical exigencies or their motives, but for their blood-curdling caucasian efficiency and monotheist single-mindedness, a raw survival talent and explosive independence that is still here when the coal strikes are on or the blood runs bad or the wife takes a powder over the ridge. It might be called "the Wetzelian."

Lewis Wetzel and his family were classic specimens of the ilk. They came to the Wheeling, West Virginia, area, restless and rankled, from Virginia proper and soon Lewis and his brothers came to represent the utmost of frontier *realpolitik*. Indian resistance was high during the 1780s (Lewis's father was killed by raiders in that decade) and Indian hunting soon became Lewis's fulltime avocation. Ranging out from the Wheeling vicinity, he sought out, alone and monomaniacally vengeful, Indian camps far into the Ohio territory beyond the Ohio River. He was merciless and miraculously efficient from the age of 16 when he killed his first Wyandot or Shawnee. Ghostlike in the forest, Wetzel would slip away from the thin-rooted settlements and disappear for days into the mountains, moaning like a painter-cat, sleeping in caverns or hollow trees, hunting Indians.

He became, early on, a legend, and also an abscesslike embodiment of his time and culture. He has been described (there are several biographies from over the years since his death in 1808) as: tall, with muscular arms and shoulders, a small head, black piercing eyes from a long spare face, high cheekbones, swarthy complexion pitted by smallpox, ears pierced and bearing silk tassles, with coal-black hair to his knees. He could not write his own name. He was morose and usually silent, preferring the company of dogs and children, or better yet prowling the woods "like a wild animal." Yet, he played the fiddle, and had a chivalrous streak in him regarding white women and several times went days out of his way to rescue them from Indian captors.

He stood on the mythic magnitude of Boone and Crockett—there are ballads and poems about him ("the stealthy Wyandottes tremble / and speak his name with fear" and so on). Even I heard stories of Lew Wetzel when I was a child, how he could run all day through the woods and leap sizable chasms like a deer. Lewis and Clark reportedly recruited him for their expedition, but Wetzel grew bored after a few months, or felt overly exposed as the terrain opened, and turned back east to lose himself again in the secluded hills and hollows.

Wetzel killed scores of Indians in those border wars of the '80s—foes, neutrals, even friendlies, it didn't matter much. He called his rifle, needless to say, "Old Nigger Killer." The Wetzelian, among the honeysuckle vines.

* * *

At Cumberland Gap: A Note to My Father

I climb this hill you have climbed many times, I would guess, as a college student nearby. Gradually the roar of trucks on Highway 25 straining for the summit of the gap recedes. I saw a Red-eyed vireo building its nest there within 30 yards of the highway and its din; it sings on in brilliant *Nonetheless.*

Up the duff trail through the jungle-rich hardwoods: maples; oaks red and white; witchhazel; chestnut oak; a tulip tree 10 inches in diameter stretching mast-like for the sun, rising 50 feet without a limb; a paw paw with huge banana-like leaves two feet long, suitable for serving up some honest Appalachian poi— on the underside of one a drab moth dozes.

Deerberry and bladderwort, hornbeam and hop hornbeam, saplings slender as girls, knee-high in ferns and Solomon's Seal. . . It is almost enough to recite the names to summon that deep soothing chlorophyll-green enlacement of these mountains.

At the height of the trail stands a monument marking the meeting point of Kentucky, Tennessee, and Virginia, a metal disc under a gazebo, the disc cut pie-wise into the three domains so one might play a sort of hollow geographical hopscotch. Off below the edge of the mountain the village of Cumberland Gap is partly visible through the trees; with my field glasses I can see an old-time red and white Sealtest sign hanging at a corner grocery. "Me and my gal and my gal's pap / We all raise hell in the Cumberland Gap. . ."

In a clearing nearby sassafras grows profusely. Small trees mostly, they are just coming into serious leafage. At the top of the three and four foot saplings tiny miniature versions of the handsome leaves are just out, from a quarter to half an inch long: tiny creatures fresh, bright golden/green reminiscent of Chablis in a glass. I begin to pick them with a vague plan for a native potpourri and homage, and soon the aroma is on my fingers and in the glade air. I try to find equal numbers of each of the three types of sassafras leaf—mitten, thumbless mitten, two-thumbed mitten—and press them in my bird book.

They are sweet and tangy to the nose, sharp as the coriander they replaced, ground as filé, in larders of the early South. It is a happy aroma in the warm sun. After handling and examining dozens of the delicate, perfect infant things, the three types of unvarying variety seem unarguably to represent prongs of some brain-like source, or at least solid evidence of a lingering ancient indecision. It is a beneficent aroma of great cultural potential, like that of sage in the west. (I will make a poultice of some of them and pack it on my nape and send some to all my friends and family.)

I sit down to soak in a sunny spot overlooking the north-facing mountain slope, give it up to the Dog-in-Sun traveler. Ovenbirds and Pewees are loud and clear, steady as a grandfather clock. Sunshine filters through the forest canopy, drips almost, the cathedral light finding its way through to the floor like seeping water. The forest closes around. Sicklepod, Puttyroot,

Thimbleweed.   Everlasting, Pipevine, Goatsbeard. Starwort, Leatherflower, Tickseed. Summer-sweet, Liverleaf, Sneezeweed.   Rattlesnake Master, Fleabane, Tearthumb. (The many-generationed, slow-settling process of plant-naming, like the careful discovery and sifting of their medicinal uses, the stabbing in the dark, the passing of the word, is, in dimension, to our field-guide world what B.C. is to A.D.) Poor Man's Pepper, Carrionflower, Speedwell. . . All in place.

From off in the understory comes a mild mannered little *eek-eek-eek* I don't recall having heard before: amphibian, insect, or mammal. . . It reminds me of a similar sound from the autumn woods of my boyhood, a monotonous *tock tock tock* common in the October days. We wondered upon it at great length, I remember. At one point, you were ready to pay schoolboys to track it down and identify the creature. As far as I know the mystery was never solved.

Five years ago in Colorado I began to notice a curious early summer sound from the town trees: a sound most assuredly made by an insect, and extremely common, but beyond that there was no information forthcoming. I tried to locate the source of the carefully placed little *ticks* (as of gently striking two marbles together), but the creature clammed up at the slightest approach.

For two years I wondered at it, waited for it in early June, listened to it in the municipal maples and the

49

foothill ponderosas. It had a pensiveness to it, within a set, elemental rhythm: three thoughtful, well-spaced clicks, like the tapping of a light baton on a podium, or five or six quicker ones in an almost snappy rhythm that approached archaic melody. There was a wistfulness and utter simplicity to it, a regularity as basic as surf-break, yet, we knew it had to be a song, a persistent sexual serenade from deep in the maximal apple boughs.

Finally, the third season, I did something. I approached a friend at the university museum who recognized the creature at once. It was a primitive type of cicada *(platypedia putnamae)* about an inch long, black with a bit of orange trim and the usual lacy cicada wings. My friend pulled out a specimen tray full of the things. The cicadas are sap eaters and therefore sweet of juice, he told me; their relicts are common in Anasazi feces. Apparently large piles of the cicadas were roasted and eaten like candy by those peoples.

That was that, after three years. The following June I found one at last in our apple tree and had a good view of it performing, watched its wings at work. It was painstakingly slow, even grudging, firsthand knowledge. Four years to learn and finally experience that humble creature. But it seems a milestone, somehow, solely by virtue of its classic, many-layered unveiling.

After that I saw several of them wounded on the streets and sidewalks about town, and wondered again

50

at it: what once was invisible now nearly rampant in the gutter. And then, one clinging shrinkingly, baffled, to the cap of an oblivious gentleman ahead of me in the IGA checkout line.

Six

The "Cumberlands," as Caudill uses the term, encompass most all of southeastern Kentucky. It describes both the broad Cumberland Plateau and the major two-hundred-mile-long single uplifts like Pine and then Cumberland Mountain extending along the Kentucky-Virginia border. It took a good while and a forester's kind word to figure that out. But it is a euphonious name and it resonates well on the heights of Pine Mountain near Whitesburg, with their immense vista to the northwest. That is the Cumberland Plateau proper, a massif wild and rugged sending up a welter of domed peaks and long-running aquiline ridges all the way to skyline.

It is easier to grasp the intricacies of the Appalachian topology in the leafless winter. Januaries, the million trees have a gawky, boney-kneed look against the snow tailings and duff of the wet hills. Little moves but the crow patrols. There is everywhere the feeling of deep pause and a coiling latency. It is raw and muddy landscape with a sad, sacked look. But the topography can be more readily got. The shadows are sharper, the bone beneath more traceable. (And when the leafage comes, with its cat-sure chromatic progression from the first winey blush in the tree crowns through the delicate mint/chartreuse haze of the new leafbuds, it is welcomed as a thing benign as blossom itself, so lovely and tempering it is.)

The roadside culture of the Cumberlands is challenging as well. Amenities—I mean simple home-cooked food and a table to eat it from—are almost nonexistent. The fastfood franchises have washed away most all the traditional beaneries. Larger highways are lined with near-constant stammering business enterprises interspersed with shanty spreads of steadily extending families. When the day is gray it all flickers on the edge of the sociological squalid. But then, I remind myself, I am just a traveler, I am simply passing through, looking up at the hills.

It is a mood best broken by diverting into the deeper mountains. Since Pikeville, I often consider the 2,000 botanical commodities growing among the mountain greenery. Most every verdant thing in sight must be worth at least four bits a pound. It represents a hospitable, groundwork sylvan commerce, a pre- or post-industrial survival mode wherein by some intrinsic symbiosis each person might earn just what they pluck or mattox from the mountain pharmacopoeia in any given week. I recall again now a moment back in the root buyer's office when the manager showed me a wild yam vine and explained that its root was used in a well known birth control pill and one of the young men standing nearby leaned in grinning and said, "I'd like to have a piece of that to carry in my truck."

At a high narrow backroad pass I pick up a tantalizing snatch of viola on the FM, just a snatch before the mountain interference shakes it off, but it puts a bit of Chanel No. 5 in the air. And then I am down into Harlan.

Harlan, Kentucky, is a legendary name conjuring the quintessential coal town that early this century was known for strike violence and mean streets. (At a gas station two days ago I saw an elder man with the quiet unmistakable gray in his face; his worn UMW cap read "Bloody Harlan" and stylized flames licked up from behind the lettering.) I have never been here before and I like it immediately. The town is set just off Highway 119 in the Cumberland River valley. Its core is accordingly buffered from the flash thoroughfare commerce and appears relatively undisturbed, intact. The town center is anchored by a columned courthouse on its green, around which lay concentric squares of streets. On the courthouse lawn, as always, stands an historical marker relating the burning of the building late in the Civil War; as is often the case in the border states it is difficult to determine which side set the match. On another corner a granite memorial lists the scores of names of Harlan County miners who perished in the coal fields since 1912.

Just across the street is a drugstore with soda fountain. I take a booth and order biscuits and gravy.

Above the fountain is a rude mountain mural. There is a pretty girl with tumbling waist-length bright red hair. But it is the steady rollick of the Kentucky chit chat that soon takes over—a communal dialect speech from all sides that warms and sweetens the place. Old gents joke at the counter. Three women in the booth behind me share clishmaclaver and size a WalMart ad. The pinched vowels can be hard to crack. I had a very tough time with the root man in Pikeville. As a dialect, eastern Kentucky speech is unbroken and dense—people hereabouts speak like their forbears and family and no one else on earth. Consciously wielded and happily shared, it binds the culture in a way that is almost tribal, with a braided strength that goes beyond simple environmental circumstance. It is a high amenity. Hearing it tossed and bantered in the streets of Harlan adds to the sensible, intact, even "walled town" feel of the place.

I like Harlan, and circle again through the side streets. I like her blanched brick hotel dating from the nineteentwenties and the houses on the hills around her rim. One more coffee, this time at the Townsite Restaurant. There are a handful of customers inside. A heavy and somewhat besmudged old woman sits smoking a long slender cigarette at the counter. She is obviously a regular, a bit down-at-heel, but at home with a ragged dignity. She reminds me instantly of the formidable crones who inhabit the post offices of Paris.

Today is her birthday. Someone has presented her a bouquet of festive balloons that bobs above her from the counter. She looks up at them now and then and shakes her head in theatrical disbelief. An old rascal seated behind her threatens every thirty seconds to pop them with a safety pin, then chortles into his coffee. She ignores him with a grand Cumberland hauteur.

SEVEN

Twice I saw, this morning, in the upper meadows of Clinch Mountain, high up in the open, rolling, stoney pastures, calm old men in overalls and straw hats, bracing themselves with canes, standing in the belt-high meadowgrass among grazing cattle. Simply standing at ease among guernseys in the sunny fields, observing in a casual and familiar way the family creatures they had obviously walked out a slow quartermile to see, to bask in the comforting bovine presence and to enjoy the uncomplicated chattels-on-the-hoof.

And then, down through the forest, curving and kinking, down one of the more oft-sung of Appalachian mountains to one of her legendary rivers, the Clinch, at a point where she controls an inviting valley. I stop at the bridge just south of Sneedville, Tennessee. Honeysuckle is everywhere, growing thickly up the sumac trees and forming an impenetrable snakey-looking tangle along the banks. The midday heat is dull and monotonous and so even is the throbbing cardinal song just upstream.

To the south, immediately above me, the rough edge of Clinch Mountain rises abruptly. Several miles north another prominent ridge runs to the northeast. I can just make out a firetower on its skyline. By my reckoning this height comprises Newman's Ridge, a feature faintly infamous in certain circles during the first half of the century as a late stronghold of Appalachia's most notorious minority group, the Melungeons.

The Melungeons are, or were, a shadowy group of remote mountain dwellers of mixed blood and mysterious ancestry. They were traditionally identified by their swarthy complexions and billowing curly hair and their enticing secrecy in the outer hills and hollows. They were recorded in this county—Hancock—by the very early 1800s, when they were described as "free colored." By 1840 they were "mulattos" in the registry. By 1950 there were an estimated five to ten thousand Melungeons in remote pockets of the unglaciated eastern United States.

Always a retiring, isolate group, the Melungeons were traditionally farm laborers in the mountains, a sort of lumpen, root-hog-or-die population. Self-contained, they minded their lumpen business. When they fought, they fought among themselves. When they married, they married Melungeons. Certain surnames became associated with the group in this region, most notably, Mullins, Goins, Collins, Sexton, and Gibson. Up in Virginia, their neighbors called them "ramps," after the wild leeks Melungeons reputedly ate in vast, odorous quantities. Their separateness of course led to imaginative reflection on the part of their non-Melungeon peers. Children in exasperating

moods might be threatened with permanent exile a-
mong the Melungeons.

Legend had it that the swarthy Melungeons
descended, in grand Wagnerian style, from ship-
wrecked sailors on the colonial Carolina coast. Some
Melungeons explained their background as Portuguese.
Others as "South European." A few as "mixed
Cherokee." They spread, always in compact groups, to
other parts of Appalachia; to eastern Kentucky for coal
mining jobs and to southeast Tennessee. Grayville,
Tennessee, was estimated in 1950 to be 40 percent
Melungeon, or "Goins," when that family name
became a generic designation.

Social historians, however, offer as a consensus the
theory that the Melungeons derived from mixed-blood
populations in Tidewater Carolina and Virginia in the
18th century, the offspring of slaves and assorted caucasian residents. Inhabiting a social nether-world, they
gradually drifted west to the refuge of the mountains.
A similar coastal mixed-blood group migrated to
southwest Louisiana to become known as the
Redbones. And up in northern West Virginia—
Barbour and Taylor counties—there sprang up a group
known as the "Guineas," who claimed descent from a
Revolutionary War veteran and a Delaware princess
(outsiders suggest a blending of Italian laborers and
black women just after the Civil War).

Over in Cumberland County, Kentucky, there are the "Pea Ridge people" and in Maryland (southeast of Washington) the Brandywine peoples, and up in northern New Jersey (William Carlos Williams' "ribbed north end of Jersey with its isolate lakes and valleys, its deaf mutes"), the "Ramapo Mountain people" who say they are offspring of Hessian mercenary deserters and Tuscarora wives. Scholars term such private-stock clans "triracial isolates."

I drive on into Sneedville for a Quixotic reconnoitre. There probably haven't been any Melungeons around here for decades. They all moved to L.A. most likely. I park in front of the Hancock County courthouse. Two boys loiter lightly, politely, on the corner. They look at me, politely, from the corners of their eyes. I do the same to them. A modest, even sub-life-size, statue of a shy, proud Civil War soldier stands on the courthouse lawn.

I stroll along Main Street to buy a cup of coffee in a cafe. I observe the passersby and they observe me, all from the sides of our eyes, out of shy politeness. No one appears particularly swarthy or curly-headed. I finish my coffee on the sidewalk, then walk to the post office and a run a quick check in the Sneedville area phonebook. It lists 3 Goins (they must have all gone to Tennessee), 35 Collins, 27 Mullins, 28 Gibsons, and 7 Sextons.

Back outside I grow nervous and feel a twinge of carpetbaggery. I would like to ask someone about the Melungeons, even to discover if the term is still current, but don't know the charge of the word on the local sensitivity, so I leave town and stop again at the Clinch River bridge to eat a sandwich. The cardinal throbs on. West and north of the bridge lies one of those long, narrow, patently Appalachian gardens carved out and squeezed in along the river: a blanched-red-earth corn patch 50 yards long and 25 feet wide.

I wanted to see a Melungeon, politely, from behind sunglasses, as I would like to see a Wallachian or a Walloon in Europe; simply to witness one of the rarer unhomogenized strains amid the order Primates. Down the road a few miles I will pass an old red Dodge Duster full of what I would call swarthy boys sporting dark mustachios. And later, up in Scott County, Virginia (another longtime Melungeon core area), three dusky prospects standing conversationally in a drizzle by the mountain road, gazing into a sharp ravine. A week after that I will ask my father if he had known the term Melungeon when he attended college half a century ago in the Cumberland Gap just west of here. He will recollect the word and moments later remember sitting beside a Goins girl in the Lincoln Memorial University chorus in 1929. That will get him up on the edge of his chair.

EIGHT

After an afternoon of slow back roads, I put up at a motel in Big Stone Gap, Virginia. The day has become hot and the parking lot, as I unload my baggage from the car, is aswarm with mayflies, or something like them, bobbing and dancing in a major hatch-orgy. I nap for a long hour and by the time I'm up and out it has rained briefly and the air is cool and sweet-tempered. I walk downtown in the dusk; the sky and the streets are an even cardboard gray.

Big Stone Gap has seen better days. The business district suffers from inanition and dry rot; the coal and the iron can't keep it all moving anymore. Empty old buildings; dusty storefronts with drooping mildewed blinds. This sort of umbilical fadeaway has a feeling all its own in Appalachia, a throb linked to the constant over-the-shoulder press of the surrounding wilderness. Low-key but tenacious, and in any long-run indomitable, the hungry forest waits—bramble, brake, and vine lurk and loom in the dark mountains around the human foothold, wait to snatch and reclaim any corner or junked car or vacant lot.

I walk by crusty saloons and the quick whiff of beer and Slim Jims from their doorways. A pre-Memorial Day peddler along the main street packs up his plastic flowers and artificial wreaths for the day, thinking *chop suey, strawberry pie. . .*

I stretch the legs and circle around town, to eventually pass by the preserved home of John Fox, Jr., author of *The Trail of the Lonesome Pine.* It is, in the darkness, a handsome old house with a good porch, aptly enclosed by trees and greenery. I remember his book, published in 1908, as a Zane Gray sort of tale set, of course, in the deep Appalachians, with, down one side of the mountain, the "smoke and steam" of the twentieth century and down the other "the Middle Ages." A tale of slow, cantankerous love and Hatfield-McCoy guerrilla gunfire and long melodious thoughts in the sun-sprinkled mountain woods. In the fictional days of that book, coal was still conceivable as an exotic gift, as a gem almost, of various wondrous sorts, like "cannel coal" (from *candle*), and the extra-fancy "bird's eye cannel," capable of being plucked in splinters from a cliff-face and lit like kindling to a match.

There is a tavern downtown so self-effacing I decide to pop in for a beer. I stand at the crusty bar before a gallon jar of pickled eggs steeping in a gasoline-colored brine. A youngish man a yard down the bar turns to me and nods and soon we are chatting. He is a wild looking chap of about 30: very small and lean to an extreme, with carrot-red hair and light blue eyes in a gaunt, Roman-nosed face. He has a faintly distracted, troubled look and his teeth are just on the verge of bucking. His clothes are worn and makeshift, his boots, I suspect, a size or two too big. His fingernails are bitten close on ruddy large-veined hands below muscular snowwhite arms.

He has been drinking for a while, I can see that. There is something about him both wet-fledgling and calloused. He speaks with a rough, blurty half-lisp. He is touting himself as a fighter, for no apparent reason, describing his assets in a calm objective way: "small but good," he has whipped men twice his size. Our conversation is halting and delicate as we instinctively read each other. He checks my responses to his stories with those pale, slightly glazed blue eyes. He sizes me up; I think it is a pull between my pony tail and stubbled jaw on one hand and my full set of front teeth on the other.

He was born in eastern Kentucky. His wife has left him. He has no job other than skimpy part-time work pumping gas. He lost his house trailer and then his car. It is a sad story. He inspires me to order whiskey but I hold off—something tells me I don't want to see Red with a couple of shots in him.

He recites his troubles in the same impersonal way he touted his toughness; just a few more blood-flecked feathers in his greasy gas station cap. As I watched him swagger like a cock to the bathroom, slipping a little at each step in his oversized boots, his twenty-inch waist above his buttless bantam legs, I thought he would make a good subject for a statue. Set it up harking south-southeast on that tri-state marker over in the Cumberland Gap.

I finish up and walk back toward the motel, through residential streets of resigned white houses, cozy enough and holding the line; houses just beginning to list and sigh, with dense and varied inner lives detectable even from the street. Houses with rhubarb in the yards. Houses with shifty upper-story apartments redolent of quiet and steady-drinking older men: their external stairways angle up the sides of the houses to small roofed porches and entryways with a rusty oversized thermometer by the scruffy screendoor and a dead geranium in a coffee can on the rail and a muddy footrug all balled up on the floor. These oft-turned apartments constitute non-aligned, undomesticated space, and they always remind me of the art of verse; of canned bachelor stew and empty long-neck beer bottles; of the pauperly comfort of the sheepherder's wagon and the hermit hut. And tonight they remind me of Red and his unadorned dog-tag woe.

The pavement is glistening from the rain shower as the village lights come on. And then, of a moment, I hear the Whippoorwills calling from the hills above the edge of town—one here, one there—elegant and discreet, warming up for the evening's work of gently rewinding the night world. It is salty-sweet music, pulsing over the town and into the screened windows where old women sew and television light flickers and men lie on their boney couches gazing at half-lit ceilings. And dogs commence to bark along, this dark wet night afloat and holding its own in the Whippoorwill world, raw and rough-edged and way beyond the would-be net-mesh of "Virginia" or "America" or anything like it.

* * *

Highway 160 from Appalachia, Virginia, to Lynch, Kentucky, is an archetypal Appalachian byway, a twisting, patient, heavily forested arc between two coal towns in their hard-worked valleys, towns permeated with all the subtle variations of black and gray and imbued with a subcutaneous carbonic hue, hugging the glistening black coal piles, the rainy trains and mineshafts and giant metal chutes that hold the towns in place, feed and doctor and bed them. The permeation is total and deep, even Pavlovian. Far underground or piled by the tracks off Main Street, coal, like night or water, is loved.

Every place on earth has its scent if you can find it or if you stay there long enough for it to find you. Highway 160 from Appalachia on up and over smells of coal. For 25 slow miles the faintly acrid aroma is there. It is not strong enough to be offensive; it is simply there, a part of the organism. But this time of year it is mixed at intervals with the heady sweetness of locust flower: an uncanny blend comprising the ultimate central Appalachian carburation.

There are stretches along this inner, deep-woods road where the right-of-way and bordering forest are crowded with butterflies in migration. You see them in concentrations throughout the mountains, casual flocks of monarchs and swallowtails finding and following open roadways or powerline cuts through the dense woods, fluttering high in treetops or simply winging their way just above car level along the path of least resistance; in this morning's case, simply taking Route 160 home.

I stop along the road somewhere near the state line to stretch and listen and take in a handmade wedding announcement proudly splashed in red and yellow housepaint on a large cliff face—"So-and-so and so-and-so—June 9, 1985/Married July 15, 1986." Across the way the highway guardrail has been battered and swiped and at one place smashed completely through onto a steep decline.

Way below, from somewhere down the mountain, I hear one of those custom car horns that bleats out "There'll be a hot time in the old town" at the push of a button. This one does the "Oh I wish I was in the land o' cotton" bars from "Dixie." Every minute or so I hear it again, gradually coming closer, I infer from the contorted mountain acoustics.

And then, around the starboard bend, here he is,

in a spanking clean red and white pickup, careening cavalierly around the curve. He hits the brakes when he sees me beside the road and pulls up for a conversation. He is a man about 50 with a shockingly preserved face from a classic high school annual: black hair oiled and neatly combed in a 1950 style with crisp white part-lines and a friendly, wide-open studyhall smile. He wears a white short-sleeved sport shirt with small black fleur-de-lys designs. The cab of his truck is spotless and lovingly zooted.

We talk three or four minutes. He asks me how I like these eastern mountains compared to the western versions, praises their dependable, Mother Hen coolness, and warns me of copperheads and timber rattlers. I tell him I like his mountains more each day and that I like his melodic horn. At that he smiles wider than ever in a way that makes me think he's had the toy only a week or two and indulges himself in it as a consciously silly gesture that by now, after who knows how many trips over the mountain, he is beginning to suspect.

No matter. He is epiphany and type-specimen. I caught him at his peak. Off he goes down the Virginia side, disappearing into the dappled woodlight and coal- and locust-flavored air. I hear his foolish, lovable car-song again in a few minutes, below and southeast, sending up a touch of "When the Saints Go Marching In."

NINE

Near Jonesville, Virginia—

I rested for an hour this afternoon in the handsome valley of the Powell River, at a spot where a minor Civil War action took place in 1863, when rebel troops captured a Union battalion. There are a good many Civil War markers in the mountains, for the most part commemorating lesser skirmishes, glancing blows, troop movements. The most Appalachian-flavored event I know of is U.S. Grant's deploying of Pennsylvania coal miners to apply their vocational skills and tunnel beneath besieged fortifications at Petersburg, Virginia, to plant explosives. As a political entity the slaveless Highland South was even generally pro-Union, but I suspect it was a part of the mountains' aloof sanctum to let such monstrous abstractions drift by, far below.

It was difficult, as ever, to imagine action in that sunny Powell valley, as it would be to picture swordplay on the site of Troy. The creek bottom trees were dark across the way and a bunting sang from a hedgerow. Indigo bunting song is a constant of the green valley terrain, as the Hooded warbler song is a constant of the deep mountains, and a bunting was likely singing the day of the Jonesville skirmish, as it was singing at some of the big ones like Bull Run or Shiloh. Or Antietam, the ultimate blood-drench and earthshake thus far on the continent. Buntings no doubt sang, then dived for cover and lurked below the bellow and din, bobbing up during lulls in the shelling to sing again. And they have been singing ever since, healing and resealing the air.

At one point in my life I read a good deal on the Civil War, especially, for one reason or another, on Antietam. Twenty-six thousand men dead, wounded, or missing that September day on Antietam Creek. The salient features on the battleground with the good-sounding names—the Cornfield, the East Woods, the West Woods—like topo details from some autumn-foliaged woodchuck-farmboy pastoral memory. Piled with corpses; forty-eight hundred dead.

Antietam was the first American battlefield to be thoroughly covered by photographers while the carnage was still in place: the twisted filthy bodies, the grotesque sprawls, the shit pants, the frozen, terrifying near-smiles on dead teenage boys from Michigan and Georgia. The nation loved it, these windows on the "life-like dead." The Antietam photos were a financial success for Alexander Gardener, the lensman. They brought a fascinating new pungency to the art of photography. Gardener would go on to cover Gettysburg; 75 percent of those pictures would feature bloated in situ corpses.

Other people didn't have to wait for photos. The day after the troops dispersed from Antietam, carriages of sightseers gathered from surrounding communities to tour the theatre and pluck a souvenir, despite the stench of decomposing bodies discernible a mile away. The ladies surely had their scented hankies to their noses. Still other clever entrepreneurial sorts managed to get photos without mussing their feet in the fly-mire. William Frassinito, in his book *Antietam: The Photographic Legacy of America's Bloodiest Day*, discovered that a popular photo of dead Union soldiers was actually a contrived fakery. The lights came on when Frassinito found another stereopticon shot with the same lads in the same location, this time arranged in an equally phony *en garde* skirmish position.

For two weeks I read about Antietam. The saturation eventually took a sort of voodoo turn. All that attention toward such a Guernica-like day, the gruesome photo-documents, the strain of the imagination to hold the scale of it all—after that immersion every rundown rural barn, each lonely middlewestern church, any ruinous farm sheds in fence-rowed fields all appeared as tainted and scarred battle aftermath: dumb, stunned things that had stood in open exposure to the radiation of brutal violence and mass death. Things were soured like that for a few days there; it was all "Civil War." Even the kiss at night somehow diluted and off-key. . . *Antietam*.

That passed, but even now, when I hear a bunting song on hot summer days, I often tend to envision a line of half-crouched, blue-coated musketeers advancing à la an *American Heritage* illustration.

Birdsound is one of the safer bets among possible trans-epoch connections, among the slender long-term continuities. Of any common shard between this moment and the erstwhile of, for example, Leif Erickson, the cries of gulls would be as sure as the feel of cold water over the head or the warmth of a small fire.

It is hard to understand how people can miss, or simply ignore, the nearly everpresent sounds of birds; how they cannot notice. It strikes me as an oversight equivalent to pleading ignorance of stars or lilacs. I would not feel quite right if on morning walks I didn't soon place myself—aurally—by reference to the flickers of the neighborhood and the belling of the solitaire down the block. They are outriggers, a solid woof of the commensal through the dailiness, day after day.

The importance of birdsong as an aspect of milieu can be major, once one notices at all. W. H. Hudson, in *Birds and Man*, testifies to the fastness of birdsound imprinted in one's early life. When he arrived in England from his native Argentina as a man in his late twenties, he was at first smitten with the new British birds, birds "which my English forebears had known and listened to all their lives long" (not to mention Chaucer and other memorables of the islands). But much later he began to ponder the birds he had left behind in Patagonia and the Rio Plata, the birds he had first come to know as a boy. He devised an experiment in audiomemory and discovered that, after 26 years of absence from South America, of the 226 species he knew from his Argentine days, the songs of 192 species were recallable, of which 154 rang ultimately clear on the inner ear. Those everyday songs can be as deep and strong in the heart as a native tongue or a landscape.

And there is the sheer, gratuitous musical occurrence of avian song and its teleological implications, the stuff of Monsieur Olivier Messiaen's brooding meditations: Bird songs as both wondrous and crystalline *givens* and as fragments of deist melody bobbing up from the *néant,* to be relished, and even transcribed for piano, say, at 6 a.m. just "au-dessus de Banyuls."— "There is a great contrast between the desolation of time (the abyss) and the joy of the bird songs (desire of the eternal light)."

On this continent during the 19th century there was a formidable cadre of bird observers out there who received the songs of birds with a range of response far beyond the cool, if not anemic, interpretation it gets in our present time. Mostly New Englanders it seems, they knew well how to stand under a tree and bask in the true poetics of it all on a scale that now seems almost Koranic in its breadth and pedigree of detail. John Burroughs, Bradford Torrey, and others of a bright and attentive generation, and especially F. Schuyler Mathews of Massachusetts. Mr. Mathews wrote a number of field guides at the turn of the twentieth century, self-illustrated descriptive books on eastern American wildflowers, trees, and other roadside life, as well as his classic *Field Guide of Wild Birds and Their Music* of 1905. The latter is a thoroughly inspired and unabashed work attacking, gently, the boundaries between human and ornithological realms; when he says "music" in his title, Mr. Mathews means *music*. A good percentage of the species profiles in his book comprises transcriptions of the bird's song onto musical stave and bar and, more than that, a well-grounded comparison of individual bird melodies or phrases to passages from the classical repertory, especially opera. The songs as transcribed to formal musical notation are wonderful documents (for the trans-epoch studies); the classical parallels are persistent and articulate enough to be, after one's resistance is worn down, virtuosic, less for their edification perhaps than for their dogged ingenuity.

He finds a riff from Chopin's "Impromptu Fantasia" in the song of the Yellow-throated vireo and a progression from Rossini's *Carnovale* in the Nashville warbler's song. The Warbling vireo song is structurally almost identical with the ninth bar of a Scarlatti sonata and a Song sparrow in Mr. Mathews' backyard consistently performed a passage from "La Donna e Mobile" from *Rigoletto*. Songs are transcribed with directions such as "moderato" and "con precisione" and the remarkably subtle nuancing of various White-throated sparrow songs is summed up thus:

"The little fellow sings Carmen's song in Tuckerman's Ravine under the shadow of Mount Washington, Turiddu's song under the brow of Mount Tecumseh, and the Di Provenza from *Traviata,* in the Pemigewasset Valley."

It is an idiosyncratic and devoted work, personal and confiding, as was often the case with that generation afield; even luxuriant in a mild "Song of Solomon" way.

John Burroughs wrote (to nail down one final dog-in-sun example), regarding the song of the Black-throated Blue warbler: It is "one of the most languid and unhurried sounds in all the woods. I feel like reclining upon the dry leaves at once."

* * *

I made a slow hibachi polenta from stone-ground meal I bought in West Virginia—strong, cows-in-the-corn, greeny-tasting meal—and doused it with parmesan and chopped scallions, ate it at sundown in the shotgun seat of the car.

And now, this daybreak in the western Virginia mountains, the dawn chorus of birdsong swells and builds until the sheer unbroken volume of the phenomenon is astounding. I end up pacing back and forth across the campsite in near disbelief at its intensity, its variety and pulse of exultation. Robins, titmice, tanagers, vireos, pewees, warblers, woodpeckers, grosbeaks—all leaning into it simultaneously at top voice as the first daylight appears. It has the implacable, insistent roar of oxygenated flame.

Or perhaps it is simply that the message is clearer, for me, this time: This is the critical imprint hour, the daily moment when the very identity and creature-form is driven home to the nestlings via the tympanum. This is the moment they receive their life-instructions and roles within the species matrix. It is a hot-blooded bio-roar, an event comparable in pitch and beauty (it extends at this instant from Florida to the tip of the Gaspé) to the great photosynthetic hymn of these mountains in their brilliant October color. An exultation of such choral grandeur and frontal plea that it must surely register on some interstellar radar-ear as a major earthly wonder and energy vortex worthy of great note.

TEN

Route 23 runs from Florida to upper Michigan, but in folklore and song she is an Appalachian-rooted road with a heartful of Appalachian connotations. She is a rough, smelly, grinding highway as scores of trucks haul their goods up and down the steep grades between Asheville, North Carolina, and Portsmouth, Ohio. To the minds of mountain folk she epitomizes egress and northbound exit, the beeline to Columbus and Detroit for bigtime flatland jobs. And when the chillbumps set in, she is the artery home.

On this stretch of 23 at Rice Bend, Tennessee, today's major tonnage appears to be scrap iron. Dump trucks, pickups, and longbed semis blow by, all loaded high with rusty scrap of cast-off machinery and hunks and parts from God knows what outmoded tool or engine. As commerce it has a raw and elemental look, like the other groundfloor Appalachian commodities: chunk coal, of course; raw furs; ginseng baled and bound for the Far East.

Route 23 is mostly a four-lane autobahn by now (though there is a sizable stretch north from Jenkins, Kentucky, that is still a two-lane remnant passing neighborly within feet of front porches and junked cars, with footbridges at her very curb). Through the mountains she is lined a good bit of the way with a touch-and-go sort of bazaar. It resembles a sooty rainy-day midway or long thin market-fair stretching single file through the hills. Aside from the villages that are gathered in 23's wake and the more conventional road-side stands aflutter with Confederate flags, roadside homes often have shocks of second-hand clothing for sale in the front yard. At an isolated gravel pull-off, a single car will sit all day beside a rack of dresses and assorted trinkets arranged on TV trays; a girl sits in the car smoking and listening to the radio; the music makes it 30 yards up the hill above her before it bleeds into the deep green kudzu. A sign on the huge trash dumpster nearby reads "No Scavenging."

And there are continual flea markets along the highway where you can browse among hubcaps and used "Playboys," microwave ovens, van seats, hideous ceramic figurines, bric-a-brac glassware, and grisly "The South Will Rise Again" towels featuring a skull with a bloody saber and a rebel flag.

I stopped at one this morning—eight tables set up in a coal-gray gravel pull-off where 23 squeezed between a small river and the Louisville-Nashville rail-road bridge. It was a fine morning and I strolled around the bazaar and back to look at the river running a kind of olive-gray below the sharp wooded hills. These traders were largely full-time marketeers, moving from place to place about the area on certain days of the week: itinerant peddlers. A person could probably buy almost anything from one of these out-fits, if they put the word out, from a live coon to young whiskey or a dead jackass. Stereos, black velvet paintings, countless Elvis caricatures. Cheap oil lamps, a three-piece sofa. "For sale, for sale." One vendor has nothing but axes.

There is a quiet old gentleman sitting patiently on the gate of his pickup camper nearby, observing like myself. We chat in the damp sunlight. He is a solitary, spends his winters moving from campground to campground in Florida state parks. Now he is slowly heading back to his native Kentucky. Last fall, he confides grimly, someone torched his little cabin in the rural Cumberlands. But he is calm. He's pretty sure he knows who did it—young anomics. One of them has already been struck and killed by lightning.

* * *

I wonder about the name "Rice Bend"—whether it springs from a grassy twist in a river, or a homestead of the Rice family, or an erstwhile switchback in a mountain trail . . . or just something like Bean Station, over south of Sneedville. I assume someone in the village knows.

The hills are larded with provocative place names. Bath and Cumberland, Armagh and Derry cast obvious backward glances. Many are simply odd—villages like

Ben Hur, Dwarf, and High Hat, Man, and War, and Aflex. The ones that intrigue me most are those whose original referents are tantalizingly hazy. Not merely humorous or soda-jerk quaint, they hang on the very edge of concrete meaning. Often they seem to be based on a geographical or natural feature, the sort of base that is especially vulnerable to corrosion as land-use and land mentalities change from generation to generation.

These words in decay remind me of the passage in Proust wherein Monsieur Brichot discourses on the ancient toponymy of Normandy, deciphering the crooked old place names strange to the eye and reconstructing their original sense. Again, they often tie into a simple topographic feature, though over the centuries the evolution of the various local tongues had worn away recognizable roots. "In the name of a brilliant diplomat, d'Ormesson, you will find the elm, the *ulmus* beloved of Virgil, which has given its name to the town of Ulm. . ." In M. Brichot's examples we discover that Cliptourps derives from the Norman *cliff* and *thorp,* village; Carquethuit from *Carque,* church, and *thveit,* a clearing—and so on and so on, well into the dinner party.

I sense that kind of latent dislocation in the mother-tongue when I see Kentucky names like Mouthcard, Wolf Coal, Thousandsticks, Head of Grassy, and here in Tennessee, Cross Anchor, Hornbeak, Soddy Daisy, Flag

Pond (just north of here on 23); even Laurel Bloomery. And when I hear them in the mouths of locals they sound susceptible, exposed on the verge of a growing gap between what they meant at one time and what they trigger here and now.

It is different with the many Indian names in the eastern mountains; although many of those etymologies could probably be traced, they are basically just unknown words to current inhabitants. But when I see Banner Elk, North Carolina, I wonder just what we're missing.

Up in Williamson, the man at the motel called the Marrowbone mine *marbon*. Down in Winn Parish, Louisiana, the Dugdemona River was at one time the Duc de Maine River. I can envision over the next century "Thousandsticks" melting down on the Kentucky palate into something as mysterious and unfathomable as Carquethuit. Then some patient etymologist will open it with his mental escargot fork and dislodge a semantic morsel from the upper Kentucky River territory of 1825 and smile fondly.

* * *

Structurally defined, the Appalachian mountain system extends from western Newfoundland to Alabama, then dives beneath the surface of the Gulf Plain, to reappear in the Ouachita Mountains of

Arkansas—and then once more in drastically altered personality as the uplifts of the Marathon Basin in west Texas (a titanic, if tenuous, prefiguration of the Appalachian source for much of the Texas panhandle speech patterns). When geologists refer to the main Appalachians as the most elegant chain on earth they are extolling their unusual regularity of form, their stability and classic exemplification of orogenic principles as much as their esthetic appeal. We are among mountains so structurally pure that some of the basic theorems of folding and faulting were developed through study of their build.

The Smokies are to the Appalachians what, perhaps, the Sangre de Cristos are to the American Rockies: a striking range within the whole that stands with a form and character entirely its own. It is not just the "smoke" of misty mornings; other mountains have that. Nor the size: Mount Mitchell to the north is higher. The Smokies from afar possess a certain drama in their general lay. There is more poise and profile to their cluster than in their neighboring ranges. Compared to other major mountains like Clinch and Roan—long, lumbering ridges—the Smokies have more arch and backbone; more a sense of "striking the pose"; more keel. They are full of hazy blue moodiness and dreamy ancient beauty. From afar they dance and flicker with a thousand secret nooks and hollows and countless half-hidden sweet-smelling things.

They represent the heart of the greatest mesophytic forest on earth, the centerpiece of the most extensive broadleafed forest in the world. The large deciduous forests of Europe and central China don't, they say, compare. What is known as the core of this phenomenon occurs in eastern Tennessee, eastern Kentucky, southwestern Virginia, and this part of North Carolina. This core forest was never touched by the glacial advances; the core and its vegetation remained stable, retaining its remarkable biologic diversity. Later, according to the "core dispersal" theory of Ms. Lucy Braun, this region served as fertile source for the reseeding of the great upper eastern forests after the glaciers' retreat. To the north spread beech, maple, and birch, species suited to the cool post-glacial clime. To the east crept oak and chestnut. Westerly, more drought-resistant trees: hickory, elm, oak, some sycamores.

Those repopulated regions are, to this day, each dominated by 2 or 3 tree species. The core forest, in contrast, has a staggering mix of trees and shrubs. In the richest areas of the Smokies botanists record 25 species as common, with another 25 present and thriving. It is a distinction not only in number; many of the core-forest species bloom with lavish blossom—a reflection of the unbroken tie with a luxuriantly flowered past.

It is at least as revealing to sit in one of the Smokies' deep forest coves as it is to stand on her peaks. It is to mull among the giant boles. In Cade's Cove the tulip trees are in flower, their brilliant apparatus one of the heights of the "lavish blossom" theory, and the silverbell blooms. The coves hold the richest of the Appalachian soils. Maurice Brooks tells the story of men cutting giant white oaks in various Appalachian coves during World War 2, when there was an urgent need to build oak-hulled minesweepers for the task of locating floating magnetic mines. The big trees were cut into 40 foot logs and trucked to Parkersburg, West Virginia, for squaring, then on to Ashtabula, Ohio, where they were kiln dried. Eight days after they were felled in the southern mountains they were part of a floating vessel on Lake Erie.

The dark murk and moist clefts of the inner Appalachians hold some of their distinctive life forms. These mountains are the best salamander study-grounds in the world. Certain lungless salamander types probably originated here in these seeps and streams and clammy caverns. Nearly each southern Appalachian mountain mass has yielded its own endemic species or race—the result of long-isolated peaks and ridges. New species still turn up now and then. A few years ago, larking schoolboys captured a previously unknown species, breaking that million-year-old coolwater dreambubble.

The humus layer in the coves (the maritime overtone of the term is apt) is deep and moist and spongy beneath the oaks and hemlocks. It gives them their air of cool distinguished wisdom and worn, almost elegiac knowingness. It is as soothing to the hands and restful to the brow as the Cumberland Gap sassafras poultice. It is the working, usable past, the past (as Francis Ponge has it) "not as memory or idea, but as matter." It has the salamander touch and sense of figure 8 and the restorative blue-sky, deep-sea calm of the blinking newt.

* * *

Looking south from the Smokies I think of solitary William Bartram on his horse, laden with specimen cases, just edging into the Appalachians from what is now South Carolina in the spring of 1776. As an absorbent botanist and flexible man he made a good enough connoisseur for an early description of these ranges.

Bartram's few days in the actual mountains of the upper Tennessee River country afforded the gamut of first-impression emotions: astonishment at the sumptuous variety of the vegetal world on these slopes; admiration for the tantalizing, everchanging hue and lure of the receding ranges ("towering mountains seem continually in motion as I pass along"); and the chill of the humid loneliness, the deeply corridored desolation of his trek.

His 400 pages of steady, quarter-profile monolog are filled with sensuous and enthusiastic detail, accounts of "exuberant pasturage," "sweet meadows" and "mountain vegetable beauties." His style conveys the bated-breath exhilaration of the daily possibility, if not probability, of cataloging a species new to science. The book attains, in the words of Thomas Carlyle, a "floundering eloquence."

The raw materials of Bartram's account of the New World's inner sanctum would turn up in the closed-eye imagery of Coleridge and Wordsworth, both of whom relished the *Travels* and apparently tapped them when seeking a dreamy supra-English landscape for poems like "Kubla Khan" or "Ruth." It is not so difficult to fit the southern Appalachians with Coleridge's "forests ancient as the hills" timbered with "incense-bearing trees" and watered by "streams of nectar." And the American youth speaking in Wordsworth's "Ruth" conjures "plants divine and strange / that every hour their blossoms change" and even what seems to be the magnolia tree in an eden-like setting.

Most of Bartram's wanderings were south of the mountains, but the Appalachians struck him full. He emerges as an unusual, companionate man with his eyes properly connected to his heart. (Every few pages he breaks into an outpouring of Latin binomial nomenclature as if reverting to his first and dearest tongue.) There is something reminiscent of Basho in

Bartram's quest, his slow, esthetic wandering, his usually solitary mode of observation, and even the damp, cove-bound moments of his "lonesome pilgrimage." Like Basho, he was *on duty* and sharp-eyed, through a "world of mountains piled upon mountains." He relishes the occasion when a lush wild strawberry meadow dyed his horse's feet and ankles crimson. The immense and regular perspective of the ranges as seen from high points Bartram compared to "the great ocean after a tempest" and (in a change of scale that renders a wonderful proto-inscape) to "the squama of fish."

The reverential traveler. And then, page 289, the Cherokee girls showed up afrolic on the streambank with bowls of fresh-plucked wild berries.

ELEVEN

There is something likeable about Cherokee, North Carolina. I felt it when I passed through 20 years ago and now again today. Its onetime tacky tourist attractions have the soft worn edges of four or five decades and an outmoded look that makes them liable for nostalgic second glances. Compared to its flagrant competition across the Smokies, Gatlinburg, Tennessee, Cherokee has an experienced grifter feel that almost amounts to character.

The absurd 30-foot-tall Indian figure beside the main street has patina enough to stand there without flinching. There are bored "Live Bears" padding endlessly in antiquated cages, free for the gaping. An old-timer in overalls dozes outside on a folding chair. Even a good percentage of the crapulous souvenirs in the various shops appears to have been hoarded about 1949. The two matching Cherokee men in garish Boy Scout-style regalia who pose exhortingly on elevated stands, one on each side of the street, are shyster period pieces in mirror image.

But there are Bartramesque delicacies to be found among the crapola. Local honey, stone-ground meals, produce from the area are sold at streetside stands. I choose the peanut man. His sign reads "Peanuts—

boiled, fried, roasted or raw." It's the boiled goobers I'm after, a rendition I've heard of but never tried.

The proprietor has a big-time set-up rigged a few yards from his counter. A sizable log fire simmers a blackened, horizontal converted oil drum full of bushels of peanuts-in-shell. He cooks them 9 or 10 hours in there, then transfers the batch to a large cast iron kettle over a perfunctory bed of coals. They sell for $2 a quart, $3.50 a half gallon.

I order a quart and he dips them out with a hand-made dipper (a kitchen pan with holes punched in the bottom). "Women always like the boiled," he informs me. "You better take some home to your wife."

They are very good indeed. They taste like well-done kidney beans, as a legume well might. It is slightly exotic to shell a peanut, even a soggy one, and find a bean therein.

They are very, very good, just as they are, although I sense they might be at their best eaten with more ceremony, langorous isolate ceremony, shelling a few into a bowl and dousing them with vinegar and raw onion, with cornbread sticks and thin beer, up in one of the lesser known ranges in the neighborhood, like the Snowbirds, or the Nantahalas, or the Unicois southwest of here.

* * *

I am not doing it justice on the page, the still poise and bearing of these forests, the lush buoyant cool of the coves. Here among the Smokies I go out four or five times a day to walk off into it, to sit, to get it on the skin.

A small cairn for the salamanders each on its proper mountain—the red-cheeked, the Yonahlossee, the black-chinned red—dozing cool as cream beneath their carefully rotting logs.

Humus strong as snuff—rappee—strong with the tang of the great respiratory Rise and Fall, snowflake and sea.

Thoughts, under these trees whose blossom-seasons extend uninterrupted back to the Jurassic, of titillative Cherokee stories of the "old days" when giant birds flew these mountains, giant yellowjackets carried off deer through these gaps. . .

TWELVE

Past Asheville (in 1964 we prowled inarticulately about the Thomas Wolfe house there for half an hour and stood briefly at the O. Henry grave); through Boone, North Carolina; to Galax, Virginia. The latter name derives from a white-flowered plant of the open southern woodlands.

On the sidewalk downtown I pass a dark, powerfully built woman of enormous sexual stature—a brooding, deeply anchored Anglo-Saxon woman in a tight print dress and high heels, she stands, emanating the Truth of the Matter with her arms crossed on her belly, waiting for two incongruous chatty men in plaid sport coats—and farther on, in a small park, I discover an extended family of gleaners combing the green lawn with metal detectors. The adults wear camouflage clothing, each wandering about with his or her machine. Kids run hither and yon to see what's unearthed when one of the things squawks and the handler kneels to probe in the grass with a jackknife. They all call gleaner things lazily back and forth through the quiet latter afternoon light. Their old Ford pickup stands at the curb with a carton of Viceroys on the dash and the reedy, syncopated beepings of the scattered detectors sound for a moment like the tuning of a small footloose orchestra.

No call for caged singing-crickets around here: from the motel, again, Whippoorwills whistling down from the hills.

* * *

The Blue Ridge Parkway is a highway preserve, 500 miles of discreet, lovely passage through the upper mountains, restricted to non-commercial traffic at 45 miles per hour. It is silent and soothing to an extent that is nearly Disneyesque in its other-centuryness and "Let's pretend" ambiance, says the cynical traveler (the same traveler who contends that the Appalachians are exactly like everywhere else in this country, except muggier and bushier and hillier, with more snakes and a can of Orange Crush on the side).

But along the parkway, nonetheless, grows a tree unusual on the eye. It resembles the locust or the catalpa, but its profuse and voluptuous panicles of bloom are a handsome lavender. I finally find it in a ranger station fieldguide. It is Paulownia, introduced in the 1830s from China, also known as the Princess tree. In China and Japan the wood is used in cabinet-making and string-instrument construction; its blossoms grace the badge of "the Japanese Order of the Paulownia Sun"—and I wonder if local dulcimer makers have discovered it yet.

* * *

I stop for lunch at a widespot overlooking some western Virginia stream, perhaps a feeder of the Laurel River. I build a baloney sandwich and eat it quickly so I can move on to my daily dose of sourwood honey from the quart mason jar I bought in Cherokee.

At roadside stands in the mountains the sourwood honey is normally kept in a place of its own, segregated from the lesser honies as a salute to its uniqueness and mystique. The sourwood is a modest, crooked, nongregarious little tree common in the Appalachians. Its chemical makeup contains enough oxalic acid to render its midsummer honey a piquance that is strong at first, startling almost, and eventually irreplaceable. Its color is a radiant amber. To my tongue, its flavor has a definite sinewy *whang* that hints of buckskin and maybe even gunpowder. Compared to the tulip tree's darker, heavier yield and the basswood's mild light honey, sourwood has the wild evasive flavor that calls one back again and again for what I can only call a *belt* or a *slug*.

Like ginseng and golden seal, wild honey has long been one of the precious bounties of the Appalachian hills. It is easy to conjure a Wordsworthian image of the early breed of Appalachian men who, inspired one well-lit spring morning far from home, devoted their lives to the search for and cutting of the wild comb.

Solitary lives of roaming the woodlands in the good seasons, plucking herbs and garnering wild apples along the way. Rarely, such men surface; there is a memorable one in Fenimore Cooper's *The Prairie*, a beeman who can almost be envisioned as a shadowy tenor in a frontier-set opera. But of course there have been pure, unbroken lineages of beehunters passing on the arcane lore and techniques of the work.

In the old days the work of attracting and lining bees back to their comb-filled trees was a specialty. The basic gear consisted of a scent (an aromatic attractor such as oil of anise or of sweetclover), a yard-square piece of cloth to sprinkle it on, and a pint of sugarwater "bait." In certain seasons salt is used as an attractor. The idea is to draw in bees by spreading the scent-saturated cloth on a bush where it catches the wind. A leafy bough is cut, laid beside the scent and sprinkled liberally with sugarwater. The bees will arrive, gravitate to the bait, gather a load and fly off toward the beetree. The hunter determines the basic route, moves his operation a hundred yards in that direction and repeats the process. Eventually he will discover the tree and look for the small telltale hole in the maple, beech, or hickory. Beemen have taken as much as a hundred pounds of honey from a single tree. It is hard to think of a vocation so unfettered and sky-struck, so full of long quiet days on intimate terms with the elementals: honey, salt, and water, insect and flower.

So after the baloney sandwich I get out the honey jar and a slice of pumpernickel and load it with sourwood and a nice chunk of comb. I nibble and sniff it in the company of a flurry of chickadees moving along the hillside, tumbling overhead in a little cloud of varied song, that assortment of calls, whistles, and high-spirited chatter that has bestowed a curious tale or two on the chickadee family over the centuries.

Certain Native American traditions passed down a detail concerning the chickadee that must be among the more esoteric morsels of lore and protoscience. They related, simply enough, that the chickadee's tongue changed each month of the winter and that a person so-inclined could compute the advance of that season by catching a chickadee and counting the branches of its tongue. Some mythological characters kept a chickadee at hand for that very purpose. During the first moon of the cold time the bird showed two tongues; during the second, three, and so on, until the break of spring, when it reverted to a single tongue.

An old story, stark and factual enough to arouse scientific curiosity, but it also raises the poetic antennae regarding the story's inception and base and crystallization in the non-industrial mind. A likely source, the bird's widely various vocalizations, its "many tongues," is only partially satisfying: The chickadee's calls and songs are not especially related to season, in my experience, not even the so-called "spring song." It is the radical leap from probable cause to mythic theorem that is baffling.

Maybe it is just another tomfoolery on the order of the snipe hunt, or the goatsuckers at the goats, or the crotch cricket. Or the bit of backwoods biology (of who knows what Appalachian ancestry) passed on by an elder fur-buyer of my acquaintance: "The possum has a forkèd dick and breeds by plugging it into the female's nostrils."

Fruits of the great human idling, of droning collective afternoons with low fly-buzz in the air and nowhere to go. A *counter-science*. Products of the half-conscious mental cud-chew hatched from broad daylight to take form, break off, and float teasingly away.

* * *

Someone in the Appalachians has a compelling propensity for naming highways and byways and bridges. Many of these features, even minor ones, are dedicated to the memory and service of someone, such as the "Jess Peterson Memorial Bridge." Up in Wetzel County, West Virginia, there is the "Lewis Wetzel Trail" commemorative route, and eastern Kentucky has its "Loretta Lynn Highway," but most often I don't know if these personages were mining heroes, World War II casualties, or just hardworking local politicoes.

But today I am honored to be rolling along on U.S. 58, the Jeb Stuart Memorial Highway west of Galax, Virginia. It is an altogether different sensation to be on the Jeb Stuart Highway, threading among the dozens of dead possums, than to travel, say, the Dwight D. Eisenhower Memorial Highway or to cross the Kosciuszko Bridge, and it is not because of the possums. There is something about a memorial to a defeated leader in one's own country that is chilling, cross-grain, almost wistful on tender American skin. The feeling is common in the South, and especially strong in the city of New Orleans among the statuary of a vanquished army—Jackson. Beauregard. Lee. It is witness to a surrendered thing. It changes the light and the sweet talk and the look of the people in the streets, and it is here today on the Jeb Stuart road.

This western Virginia is a seductive, idyllic landscape of moderate mountains and a well-rooted human population. Homesteads along 58 appear as inviting and sensible as any dwellings I know: Old white frame houses on shady knolls; plenty of open pasture; sizable gardens near at hand; and the enormous buffer and beauty of the forest all around and up the hills. People sit on their porches amid their hounds beaming an aura of comfort with character; of hard-won patience; of, let's say, peach jam.

It has occurred to me, traveling through these hills, that the density and closure of the mountain

103

terrain and the heavy forest might tend, speaking of psychological space, to restrain or subdue—cut—the horizontal impulses and nourish the more nearly vertical ones, like song and prayer and rocking steadily on the porch. Perhaps that is part of the peach jam atmosphere—a satisfaction with one's home territory that is almost palpable. In any case it strikes me now as a noble capacity, the capacity of loving place, holding place, and a high form of human excellence. It is something so deep and clearwatered that for days now I have felt that the true Appalachian moment, as far as human content goes, is the moment when people disappear into the hills, turn up a narrow hollow road, or walk back a thin lane and fade into the treedom. In a place like Nevada it is just the opposite—the revelatory moments occur as people gather at gas stations or dark cool bars, or first appear, miragelike, on the desert horizon and gradually come into solid focus.

I nearly missed the small green and white sign in the village of Hiltons, Virginia, pointing the way to the Carter Fold. Even then it took a moment to register. I knew the Carter family came from southwest Virginia—I noted it as a place called Mace's Springs—but here, obviously, we are, so I turn around and go north off the Jeb Stuart road and proceed on what is soon proclaimed the A.P. Carter Memorial Highway. North of Hiltons, past a time-free little coalyard where one can purchase bituminous by the pailfull, up a cozy valley of some Clinch Mountain spur about three miles, and there it is, the old Carter country store and family fold, preserved as a state landmark and museum.

It is late Sunday afternoon by now and the place is closed. I walk slowly around the grounds and peer in the door to see walls full of musical instruments, dresses and Sunday suits, and photos of the various Carters. Portraits of the clan in stained glass hang in the upper windows.

Someone tends the rosebush by the sweetwater well out back—the Mace's Spring?—and it is iris time in Scott County, the air is heavy with that fragrance. A herd of Simmenthals graze beyond the Carter Highway at forest edge. It's time for a soak; I lean against a tree and catch the latter sunlight and conjure a brief fiddle-tune mantra of Appalachian classics: Wildcat Whiskey, Old Zip Coon, Happy Times in Butler, Bobbed-tail Buzzard, Double Headed Train, Hawk's Nest, Whole Hog or None, Hell After Yearling, Stealin' Chickens, Billy in the Low Ground, Daddy's Pack of Hounds, One-eyed Goose, Back Side of Albany, Bung Your Eye, Chaw Roast Beef, and Cross-eyed Charlie. . . To which I add a couple of my own invention, just to link-up with those supple-wristed boys: "Possum on the Back Porch" and "Baby Ate the Bee." I take a cool drink from the Carter well and head back down toward Hiltons.

The music is as fast and deep in these mountains as wine is along the Loire, a permeation that in its heyday of the early 20th Century rendered singing *almost as universal a practice as speaking* in these hills.

They say one hundred of the three-hundred traditional British ballads reached this continent. They were singing them in the inner Appalachians—"high, rubato, and nasal"—by the first decade of the 19th Century, the Scotch-Irish and their precious portable fiddles, and the music still surges as the foremost Appalachian sweet and potent antidote to the Wetzelian. It is in the air, virtual or latent. It binds and supports the southern mountains like a geologic dike.

Singing as universal as speaking! The possibility that music *is* the human signature—not as movie score, sappy background in a silly riverboat film, but front-and-center as gist and yeast of human presence. Men and women in the streets of Galax or Ivanhoe or Raven capable of picking up a fiddle or guitar and breaking into that High and Lonesome—that tossing of the tree.

Thirteen

It is a gloomy morning as I drive back into West Virginia, back into the heart of the Appalachians. If the Smokies and their neighbors stand as the core of the great Appalachian botany, this southern tip of West Virginia is the core of the current cultural phenomenon. The clouds are low and gauzy over McDowell County as I prowl through gritty hamlets wedged into hillsides above and below the small road. They have a chilly and regretful look this morning, a shiver-like-a-dog look. Squire, Cucumber, War, Yukon.

After the Smokies region and the Blue Ridge country—the spruce, even tony side of the Appalachians—this is back to the frontier: no Winnebagos on the road, no caged bears or trained hillbillies. There is a feeling of penetration into the real mountains after a simulated training course or slide show, and it is sharp with the sting of isolation and the drop of chilly loneliness. The clouds finally work into a light needling rain. A hound trots along the highway with his tail between his legs, looks apprehensively over his shoulder at me as I drive slowly by. It is damp and cold and the occasional faces at doorways appear gaunt and full of a slow surprise; they look like Ishi, just down from the hills. It is the gooseflesh feeling of enforced loneliness, as in George Jones' high notes when the syllables twist and climb into a creaturely moan-howl *in extremis*. I think of the first Scotch-Irish settlers on days like this, huddling in the 1810, Ulster-style mud and stone huts far up the mountains with a Bible and a violin on the slab mantle and a muddy hog lolling at the door.

I stop at a roadhouse among a few huddled buildings on an isolated stretch somewhere near Wolf Pen and dash in for something to eat and some company. There is a young boy playing a pinball machine in one corner. I take a window table so I can watch the rain and the weary wipers on the cars creeping by. After looking over the menu I order the "Coal Miner Special"—a hamburger and cornbread and beans. I ask the waitress why it is called that and she explains, "Miners like to eat beans." I let it go at that. If I were concocting a coal miner special I would consider a spit of roast canaries with a side of pasta carbonara.

The rain is downright heavy by now. Across the way I can make out a feeble sign for a "Tanning Salon." If there were less rain in the Appalachians and the soils less leached accordingly, these hills would be shaved bald for agriculture, like the loess hills of far western Iowa. I remember camping one night on Mount Mitchell, right up at treeline, when a rain came in and soon developed into a blockbuster storm with an uncannily steady two-hour crescendo of wind and electricity. We finally bolted in the middle of the night; as we threw our soaking gear into the car the tent was flapping wildly from one last stake and the stunted trees were crying and slashing in the wind. We drove down to Burnsville, North Carolina, and took a motel room, slept all day and got up in time for dinner at the Nu-Wray Inn down the street. There must have been 50 people waiting in the Nu-Wray lobby. Long tables set end to end were laid with wonderful country ham and fried chicken and half a dozen steaming family-style vegetables and assorted downhome relishes. Then they rang the starting bell and we all rushed to take a seat and everyone ate so absurdly fast it was over in 15 minutes.

My coal miner special arrives and the waitress asks if I would like onion with it. She brings a small dish of thick onion slabs; it costs four cents extra and it makes a clank when she sets it at the table. There is the waitress; her girlfriend keeping her silent company at the counter; the distracted boy at the pinball machine. And the chill of the rain seeping in from outside and the strange Celtic rustle of low-tide unreality like a moss on it all—Traveler's moss.

Driving on when the rain let up, I pass an old powder blue Ford with a petite old-timer grinning at the helm. He loves his steering wheel, and has a fancy festoon of ten wet squirrel tails dancing from his outside rearview mirror, a sort of backwoods flourish I have not seen in a good while. When I was growing up

109

it was common to see garage or shed walls in the community decorated with squirrel tails in autumn, representing both a signal of modest success and, more than that, claiming a membership in the fraternity of woodsmen.

Squirrel hunting is the most contemplative of the carnivore sports and the men who are particularly and proudly squirrel hunters are different from those who go out after ducks or rabbits or antlered game. There is a passivity involved in waiting silently beneath an October sugar maple for the fox squirrels to emerge, a passivity that, after a few long seasons, imbues the hunter with firsthand knowledge of relatively subtle things. Squirrel hunters come to know the fine yet critical difference between paying attention and not paying attention, a sort of un-American sense of the distinction between seeking and not seeking, of a frequency and presence (or "non-presence") that wild creatures are the first to notice.

In my hometown you could pick the squirrel men out of a gas station crowd without much trouble. They were generally quieter, slimmer men who stood easily to one side while the meaty deer hunters told the raucous stories full of leer and guffaw. I remember especially one accomplished squirrel man who practiced the sport as an art and whose garage door was hung with several dozen squirrel tails by Thanksgiving each year. He knew patience and soft words and when

110

he talked hunting he made a nice easy gesture with one hand, representing the little jump-hops of a fox squirrel moving along the ground. He was retired and probably spent four days a week in the beech-maple woods from September to Christmas, usually alone with his .22. Such exposure seemed to give him a ballast and an inner life that the deer men blatantly lacked. The last time I saw him on a visit to that village he hailed me on the street. It was late September and the squirrel woods itch was on him. He wondered if I might go with him over to Hocking County after gray squirrels one day that week. He had had a heart attack the previous spring and was afraid, frankly, to go into the hilly woods alone since then. I felt curiously honored that day, as being singled out as worthy of, God forbid, lugging him out of the woods over my shoulder, and still do, I suppose, thinking of him now, *down there* in that Ohio town, at the very foot of these Appalachians.

* * *

Up on Highway 97 I pass several large ugly mines, including a giant National Pocahontas pit, harsh and pustular, and the big Ford and Mack coal trucks are thick on the road. They name them and I catch, as they blow by, monickers like "Big Dog," "The Legend," and "Family Tradition." East of Pineville, not far from a massive coal hole, I pull off to catch up on my notebook, lowgear up into the parking lot of the Sweet Divine Baptist Church, set on the slope above the highway amid evergreens and thick clumps of rhododendron.

Churches are rampant in the inner Appalachians. They range from well-established little chapels in the vales to a plethora of raw recent structures; some are quick cinder-block jobs, a few consist of house trailers wedged in along the road, guyed in a muddy slash. There are Freewill and Mission Bible and Free Pentecostal, Old Regular and Primitive Baptists, Churches of God in Jesus' Name and the Church of God of Prophecy. The most tantalizingly poetic so far was the Big Elk of Zion Christian Church. Small and wiry, they are common enough in the mountain land-scape to suggest a sort of spiritual plimsole line of need and bloodshot Protestant eyes. They speak of many wounded and heavy bandage, of stopping a hole in the dike.

Somehow, amid the big raw mines, coal seems a firm part of it all. Thinking of the high presence of Christian dogma surrounded by the violent coal churn, one senses a spiritual divot, a desperation that is some-how pathetically post facto. If Christian thought has ever had a word to say regarding custody of the natur-al world I have not heard it; nothing beyond the ancient "Take and Use" greenlight of the early books of the Bible. That void and lack of grounding is what stands out here amid the bandages and dispiritedness of the coal-grip and market-screwage and poisoned streams. The religious and cultural failure to extend the reach of ethics beyond the human realm, the failure to *inscape* the human presence within the larger frame, invites in the end disastrous vacancy and widescale nervous disorder.

Nothing, perhaps, that 50 or 60 per capita infant-hours of watching a waterthrush might not mend. I thought about that in the yard of the Sweet Divine and again later as I drove slowly through the hamlet of Maben. It is a lovely village and today it was perfectly bedecked amid its greening backdoor hills with great ranks of redbud trees in bloom, sycamores creamy white beside its stream, and here and there a dogwood in flower. Prime and perfect in its given daily beauty.

I thought of all the nooks and crannies in the hills I've passed the last few days, of all the private, hardly known goings-on of the inner Appalachians, the worka-day quotidien up those hollows and back those sketchy cocoa gravy roads, a quotidien as powerful and private, I have come to sense (or perhaps hope, circling amid it), as inner Kiva doings. Back those runs you will find the true Appalachian palladium, drawing its matriarchal strength from stamen and anther and far-swinging cycles. The coal with its trimmings is a circumstantial spasm and a prop; loved or not, it is a pseudo-protector, a stack of numerals to be consigned to newsprint and consumed by belching cigar-chewing city men. Up the hollows, out of sight, the true redbud Appalachian gristle goes on, tough, lean of tendril, and instinctively resistant to the washed-out flatland world.

FOURTEEN

The next day I stop at the Cranberry Glades state area in Pocahontas County for a much needed walk on the elevated boardwalk skirting the swampy forest and looping through the sunny open clearing of the bog itself. The mellow Yew Mountains surrounding are still lacey with young leafage in pale tentative tones, tender on the eye. The shadbush is blooming in Pocahontas County, their crooked little finger-blooms fragile as witch hazel. Up on the hillsides you see them, scattered smallish trees, their white blossoms hanging tenuously in the deep woods, ghostly as thrushes. Their knobby thin limbs reach meekly for a frail sunbeam striking the forest floor. Their nomenclature is as delicate as their bloom. In May it is Maybush; in June, with its delicious fruit, it becomes Juneberry. And elsewhere, when the shad run in the eastern rivers, it is Shadbush. Similarly, the wild geranium of the spring becomes Cranesbill by summer's end when its long, beaklike fruits take form. Different names for different seasons, as the humans walk by, sifting and sorting under their various compelling suns.

As I loiter at the outermost reach of the boardwalk I hear a group of young elementary children arrive in the parking lot over in the woods to begin their tour through the bog. Hidden from my view, they raise their 20 tiny voices in hoots and hollers, a chorus of falsetto West Virginia accent, like a composition in a certain winsome geographic key.

I skip the "What Went On Here 10,000 Years Ago" sign beside the trail. One hundred centuries. That's too far back—back toward the giant yellowjackets—and too round a sum. Ten thousand—the figure favored by Chinese poets in their rough estimation of forever and their quick reckoning of the human sorrows. Only recently has a single century emerged as a graspable unit complete with sunrise and sunset. I run across old shoes and a pogo stick in the attic that are, suddenly, almost half a century old. I know one-hundred-year-old trees and watch them blossom when I can, to gauge the eventual carefreedom of the thing. The lumbering brick department store on my hometown square went up in 1876—I know the workers hefted slowly breaking news from the Little Bighorn in midsummer of that year, as they climbed and carried and bantered. The same broken teeth and wind in the hair, the same nicotine stains on the fingers.

It is the overlap of generations, of course, that tames it, smooths the conceptual edge of "century." The one-hundred-year-old persons celebrated in newspapers, smiling bonily above a cake—lay a couple of those end to end and you're back to William Blake. "I never knew him, but my neighbors did."

116

Mozart, Chaucer, Pocahontas—not so far back there
on high-barometer days.

"Cranberry" derives from low German, *crane-berry*.
The Cranberry River heads here in these bogs, thence
to the Gauley, west of here, the Kanawha, and the
Ohio.

I notice on the flora checklists given out by regional
parks that there are still a surprising number of plants
that have no common name as yet. That is wonderful
news; I volunteer, will begin tomorrow, or the day after.

* * *

Midday I stopped to bird along the Guyandotte
River, pulled off near one end of a highway bridge. I
walked back a dirt road into the riverside brush, away
from the traffic and its buzz. Around a bend, well out
of sight of Route 10, I found two pickups—both new
and well-curried—nosed into the brush side by side,
heavily screened by full-blossom honeysuckle. Two
heads showed in the red truck; it was the lunch hour
and this was obviously a honeysuckle tryst, a nooner on
the Guyandotte.

I walked by with my eyes on my own business, keeping my binoculars visible as a sort of badge of explana-
tion and apology. Almost immediately as I am by them,
I hear the slam of a truck door—then again—and both

117

engines fire and back out and scram away toward the highway. I could see them at that point, through the trees, as one turned and hurried east, the other off in a roar toward the west. Vintage mountain ballad stuff, nipped in the very May-bud. And the dust settled slowly back on the honeysuckle.

FIFTEEN

I took a room in an odd motel in Buckhannon, West Virginia, run by an odd, friendly family with personalized cadillacs and large oil portraits of several generations on the lobby walls, and walked out to a nearby cafe for supper. I had a wonderful plate of pinto beans loaded with chunks of good smoky ham with good cornbread on the side and free onions.

It was a comfortable place with a large local clientele. They all ordered the sirloin tips in gravy special. After eating, I got out my pocket notebook and legal pad and began to decipher my on-the-run scribblings of the previous day while they were still retrievable. It was, apparently, a moment of the Obvious Traveler: In an uncanny synchronization, each time I lifted my hand to the pad and began to write, all the people at the large "regulars" table across the room stopped talking and looked over at me, in a nonchalant, unaggressive manner, but synchronized nonetheless. I ran a couple of test feints just to be sure, and then gave it up, and pulled out my Buckhannon *Record Delta.*

I read where the FBI nabbed a fugitive from Alabama in the Buckhannon area—a man, 47, wanted as a fugitive from charges of armed robbery, kidnapping, rape and sodomy, found well-harbored in a 21-year-old woman's bedroom. Elsewhere, a 33-year-old man from Rock Cave turned himself in for stealing a tractor from Buttermilk Hill; the tractor was recovered earlier this month from the woods on Pritt Mountain. And Dr. Andrei Anikin, an eminent Russian economist, will speak at West Virginia Wesleyan College, here in Buckhannon, in October.

Then I walked downtown and bought a bottle of Virginia Gentleman and circled the courthouse to have a look at Buckhannon (I thought the name might be an archaic form of Buchanan, but the lady at the motel told me it was named after a Delaware chief). Along the way I spied a poster for a Ham and Bean Fest at the Presbyterian Church and a rain-wrinkled old flyer from a Ramp and Squirrel Festival that took place last September—and apparently every September—on the first day of hunting season. The ubiquitous historical marker stood by the courthouse. Under the heading "Frontier Days" it announced, among other things: "To the north stood the Giant Tree in which the Pringle brothers made their home."

* * *

This morning I drive east from town, crossing the Buckhannon River, and then the Tygart Fork, and then the Laurel Fork, back into the million trees and the kink and fall of the highways. After ten days there is a handy new callous on the middle finger of my left (steering wheel) hand from negotiating the mountain roads.

West Virginia is the only state entirely within the Appalachians; one can't help feeling she is both charmed and protected by that fact, by the enormous vegetal energy of the mountains that resists casual dallying and comes storming back with shrub and vine, even after the ravening of strip mining. After ten days in the Appalachians you slowly realize you are within one of the great wild continuums of the continent, a phenomenon you might drive through for weeks or walk through for shady months without leaving the hills. It sinks in, with the locust blow and the soft deciduous textures and the "Lizzards for Sale" signs along the way.

It is anachronistic almost, for a flatlander, to see cattle in the mountains, grazing on modest pastures cut from hillside slopes and surrounded by dense woods. It is both odd and beautiful, like robins on a beach. The creatures seem different up there amid the dogwoods in bloom and blackberry edges—somehow "old world" or part of an ancestral tableau on the "domestication of animals" theme.

I cut north into the Canaan Valley, a high wind-trimmed plateau-valley that in October, when the rest of the mountains are reaching the peak of autumn color, is often seared by altitude frost. In Davis, where I stop for a horrible restaurant lunch, there are little figurines carved of coal for sale at the cash register—choo-choos and black bears. And then east on Highway 93, I am officially into the West Virginia panhandle.

I want to get off into hinterland, so I stop to study the terrain (the governor, Mr. Gaston Caperton, who is pictured on the state map, has a pleasant, wide-open, almost provencal look to his face) and choose the little road going east out of Scherr—I believe they call it the Greenland Gap road. Immediately there are no more coal trucks and we are into a whole new swim, bucking cross-mountain, over the ridge, twisting up through the dense forest and into massive rocky upthrusts and boulder fields. It is a 20 mile per hour road and a challenge at that, so distracting and lush is its passage and moist wilderness. I pull over at one of the high spots to decipher a small tin placard tacked on a roadside tree, an elderly, handpainted sign in weak white paint: "Wreck of the old 53 Plymouth."

And then I stop at a point in the deep woods, one of those dark and damp secret spots along a small trickle of stream with high drippy ledges rising above. It is so enclosed that it is almost chilly. There are warblers singing off in the understory—Redstart, Hooded. After the proverbial ten days, the constant collective bird-voice accumulates to the point of saturation. Individual species' songs begin to blur, particular song traits to soften and to coalesce with other species' songs. It is a disorienting sensation, echoing perhaps the theoretical ancient point when all birdsongs were one, a single murky cry in the cretaceous ferns.

But the brilliant Redstarts, foraging in these deep dense woods: the nest is the anchor, the song is the rope.

Soon I am over the mountain and down into Medley, in the sunny valley of Patterson Creek. I drive north, downstream and straight away, toward the Potomac. It is another long-lived handsome valley with an abrupt mountain wall rising hard by the east bank of the stream. There are regular farms along the road and enticing dirt byways branching off into the hills. I see a Jersey cow so heavy with calf her eyes seem to water. To the far west, well beyond the ridge I just crossed, looms a long, strong mountain on the skyline.

The farther down valley I go, the more imposing the farms and their houses and the magnitude of their operations. I stop to make a sandwich at the Harness Run Church of the Brethren, pull in under a big ash tree near the neat brick chapel set in a small hollow shaved out from the woods. It is a blood sausage sandwich with mustard—*'sblood!* A Pileated woodpecker calls behind me; pretty Patterson Creek runs beyond the road half a mile. I hate the thought of giving up this pleasant road and getting back on Highway 50. I will lean in the sun for a minute before going on into Burlington. . . *The possum is the coyote of the Appalachians, with all the concordant rights and mythical irresponsibilities.*

123

Or maybe the armadillo, given the possum's penchant for highway travel and its phenomenal road-kill attrition. Either way, it has a dick of flint and reproduces by striking it against any given piece of steel.

Sixteen

I pull into Paw Paw, West Virginia, about noon. The day is overcast and vaguely expectant. Deep within, I realize I was headed for Paw Paw the entire trip; it has been an unspoken but persistent destination by virtue, pure and simple, of its name glowing on the map beside the upper Potomac. The past several days, whenever the traveling grew tiresome and the look-see thin, it was Paw Paw that loomed beckoningly on the horizon.

I had envisioned a bright, breezy day with good, tonic sunlight on the trees—but this will do. I make a brief swing through the residential part of town—old neighborhoods up and away from the river; neighborhoods of well-built, classic Appalachian houses set close to the street and low to the ground. It is a standard enough village; I like the way her railroad tracks swing with the curve of the river.

Then I drive back to the main street and stop at a cafe. It is a converted frame home, apparently, sooty white and listless—but I can't rush through Paw Paw after all that subliminal beckoning.

There are two women in the place, a clammy old cook and a young waitress. I am the only customer, again. I order cherry pie and black coffee and scan the bulletin board near the door. "Chihuahua Puppies for Sale—Father on Premises." The pie is not good, but I finally manage to interrupt the women's desultory talk and get the young one going about the block-long, acned, cream-colored factory sprawling in desuetude just across the street. It was the Vesuvius Crucible, she tells me, until that business dried up some years ago. The last she knew someone had converted its window-less metal halls to a mushroom nursery. And nowadays most everyone in town travels to work way down in Winchester, Virginia.

From the cafe I drive down to the Potomac and off on a dirt road to a little boat launch area below the new bridge. I get out the binoculars and amble down-stream, through a narrow little grove east from the bridge. Bait litter and beer cans are strewn along the bank, but no birds show themselves at the moment. Ornithologically, this is on the edge of legendary terri-tory. The three counties immediately east of Paw Paw—the three counties comprising the jagged beak of the West Virginia panhandle—were the original sites of one of the famous American mystery birds, the Sutton's warbler. This creature, suspected of being a hybrid between the Yellow-throated and the Parula warblers, was discovered in May of 1939 on Opequon Creek over toward Martinsburg. Only another half-dozen or so have been seen in the ensuing half-centu-ry, all but one in the panhandle. The bird has taken its furtive place alongside the Carbonated Swamp warbler (collected, described, and painted by John James Audubon in May 1811 and never heard of since); the Blue Mountain and the Cincinnati warblers, neither bird seen in over a century; and Bachman's warbler, the rarest songbird of late 20th century North America.

For a moment I consider the possibility of loading the daypack with peanut butter and striking off down-river to loiter at likely intersections and test my bird-luck. (Twelve years ago I spent ten high-adrenalin days on the banks of the Suwanee River *looking for*—in a rhapsody of naiveté—Bachman's warbler: up each morning at daybreak to brew a rank cup of instant coffee with tepid water from the Manatee Springs camp-ground tap and off into the burgeoning late-March woods along the river to sweep in vain the budding treetops like radar.) But no, the rain still lurks in the upper hills and the odds are way too long. I spend ten minutes along the Potomac, idling out to the large sycamore leaning at a 45 degree angle over the river, before turning back to the car.

So it seems it wasn't the Sutton's warbler that beck-oned from Paw Paw all through the preceding week, if one can track such things. There is no feast in the streets of Paw Paw or sudden full-moon epiphany; no grail it seems but the river scent. Just the katydid-green toponym aflutter on the south bank, the sweet double-

127

thump of the spondee, with hot black day-in-place coffee and a low basket full of Chihuahua pups shivering in their nest like little birds.

* * *

I cross the Potomac and set down on the Maryland panhandle driving in the direction of Cumberland. The "Maryland Panhandle" (like, perhaps, all panhandles) has always had a good sound to it, in my ear, evoking a distinctive, even rebellious geography. The vegetal life is deep oak/hickory.

I remember the city of Cumberland as possessing an attractive upstream, early morning funk comprised of hard-earned river smudge and rusty lackadaisical business. But the farther west I get from the Paw Paw bridge the more I am aware of a lessening, a diminuendo of something I have grown used to over the past two weeks. Trailer homes are replaced by sporty looking river houses suggesting bureaucrats and barristers sneaking up from D.C. to grow roses and chop wood. There is a creeping in of the Mild again, a non-Appalachian grip and grooming with the feel of bluegrass or piedmont Virginia.

Just outside the village of Old Town I see a sign advertising Tennessee Walkers for sale, then a fine berry-roan herd of shorthorns in a low-slope pasture-opening. I need to slow it down a little, slow the lessening, not to get the geographical bends, so I turn off the main highway and drive into Old Town. The town sits a few hundred yards from the river and, from the evidence of the Michael Cresap House where I park and get out, is old enough. Mr. Cresap lived in the chipper stone home from 1742-1775 and fought a war in the Ohio Territory that carries his name—the "Cresap War" against the Indians up there. At the start of the Revolution he led a band of crack panhandle riflemen painted up Indian-style to Boston to offer their services against the king.

I want to listen a bit here, shadow around a little and listen for the local accent, this spot being the closest I will get to the mythical south-central Pennsylvania culture-hearth of the Scotch Irish, from which they spilled into the more southern mountains. A man talking on the sidewalk sounds vaguely and brusquely Brooklynese. No one else is out and about, so I stroll down toward the river, stopping for a moment at the old mill on the canal that parallels the North Potomac (the river has forked between here and Paw Paw; I believe this branch is considered the main stream). There are birds in the trees but they are jumpy and elusive.

I follow a minor road to the river and find there is a toll bridge at the crossing, with a small toll booth set above a single-vehicle span handmade of planks and railroad rails. The Potomac isn't more than 30 yards wide at this point, I would guess, moving along at a nice clip between Maryland and, across the way, more West Virginia.

The woman operating the toll booth has an odd though unobtrusive speech; certainly not a strong "mountain" twang or pinch to it; more of a congenital throatiness with an odd gallumphing lilt in it and a hint of washed-out drawl. The bridge is a private family enterprise that, like any other small business, has changed hands now and again over the decades. She discusses the ravaging flood they had here some years back and tells me "You can walk down to the river if you want to, but if you set foot on the bridge it's 20 cents."

I figure it is well worth the money to get back to West Virginia for a few minutes, especially in this unexpected pedestrian way. I pay up and wander on down to the bank. A large lone datura plant grows on a hummock near the water, elegant, fulsome, preening and bobbing to the tune of the river. Up and downstream there are big red maples crowding the banks with an occasional slim sycamore shining among them. I cross the bridge and stroll into a grove of West Virginia hackberries near the abutment and sit down for a grand finale, a mull and decompression before I leave the southern mountains, while a flock of crows harass a hawk downriver. I have a Grimes apple I bought yesterday in Romney, West Virginia. Romney, the sign at the courthouse said, changed hands 56 times during the Civil War.

Day long/century short. Next time through I'm going way on down, down through the Unicois and farther, to turn around in Young Harris, Georgia. I'm going to choose one of those secluded ledgy knobs somewhere in the outer mountains, climb it and sit for a day or two to partake of the enfleurage. I'm going back to the Nu-Wray Inn in Burnsville and eat for an hour this time.

Right now, here on the Potomac bank, I would say the most memorable emblem of the past two weeks—the most oddly and touchingly lighted detail—is the pathetic little placard commemorating "the wreck of the old 53 Plymouth."

And then I find myself recalling the dead Black-throated Blue, its quarter-teaspoon of bonedust for the Appalachian ossuary. And the scores and scores of blooming redbuds. I think of foggy-day Anglo-Saxon words like *slag* and *eft*, *coal* and *newt* and *sty*—syllables irreducible as stones in a river. And I wonder about Green Spring, West Virginia, a village just around the roadbend from where I sit; less than a mile I would guess from the map. The Generous Traveler imagines her a nice one, aged and settled like a spry cheddar. . .

But prose or mull can't really touch it, not for a grand finale. Only song will do. I'll go back to the car and play something right, something sunburnt and yeomanly and dancing-transcendental: "Red Pig" by Kyle Wooten.

And then a little acid rain begins to fall.

Works Consulted

Lewis Wetzel, Indian Fighter. C. B. Allman. Devin-Adair, 1977.

The Appalachians. Maurice Brooks. Houghton-Mifflin, 1965.

The Birds of John Burroughs. Ed. Jack Kligerman. Hawthorn, 1976.

"Country Music and the South." George O. Carney. Journal of Cultural Geography 1 (1980).

Night Comes to the Cumberlands. Harry Caudill. Little, Brown, 1963.

The Trail of the Lonesome Pine. John Fox, Jr. Grosset and Dunlap, 1908.

Antietam: The Photographic Legacy of America's Bloodiest Day. William Frassinito. Scribner's, 1978.

Birds and Man. W. H. Hudson. Knopf, 1916.

A Guide to Medicinal Plants of Appalachia. A. Krochmal, R. Walters, R. Doughty. U.S. Department of Agriculture, 1971.

The Folk Songs of North America. Alan Lomax. Doubleday, 1960.

Fieldbook of Wild Birds and Their Music. F. Schuyler Mathews. G.P. Putnam's, 1905.

"Melungeons." Edward T. Price. Geographical Review 41 (1951).

Appalachia: A Regional Geography. Karl B. Raitz and Richard Ulack. Westview Press, 1984.

Photo: John Deason

Merrill Gilfillan was born in 1945 in Mt. Gilead, Ohio. He attended the University of Michigan where his poems were awarded a Major Hopwood Prize. He studied with Ted Berrigan at the University of Iowa Writer's Workshop (MFA, 1969). He is the author of seven volumes of poetry. His first collection of essays, *Magpie Rising: Sketches From the Great Plains,* received the PEN Martha Albrand Award for Non-fiction in 1989. His volume of stories, *Sworn Before Cranes,* was awarded the Ohioana Fiction Award for 1994. He makes his home in Boulder, Colorado.

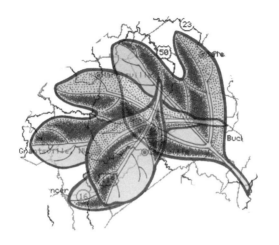

Profile Series

The Desires Of Mothers To Please Others In Letters
Bernadette Mayer

Heart Of The Breath (Poems 1979-1992)
Jim Brodey

Burnt House To Paw Paw: Appalachian Notes
Merrill Gilfillan

Series Editor: Michael Gizzi